Arlon F
Trier FS*
Meuse
Mosel
Reims FS
Metz FS
Rhine
Châlons-sur-Marne FS
Laye S
Paris FS
Marne
Nancy FS
Bouray F
VOSGES
Portieux F
artres S
Troyes FS
Epinal FS
Euffigneix F
Seine
Vix
Orléans S
Châtillon-sur-Seine S
Vertault F
Schaffhausen
Rhine
Basel S
Mandeure F
Seine-Quelle F
Windisch F
euvy-en-Sullias F
Brugg S
Alise-Ste-Reine FS
Dijon FS
Malain F
JURA
La Tene
Bern S
Bourges
Muri F
Autun FS
Mont-Beuvray
Saône
Avenches FS
Allmendingen F
Boscéaz-Orbe FS
Moudon
Prilly F
Visp F
Nyon F
Genf S
Guéret S
Martigny
Vichy S
Loire
Rhône
Nouaillaguet FS
Allier
Lyon FS
Martineiche FS
seix FS
CENTRAL
ALPS
Vienne FS
Les Cars
Neschers F
Grenoble
MASSIF
Rhône
Durance
Bozouls
Montsallier F
Rodez
Mondragon F
Vaison FS
Sisteron FS
Puech-Réal F
Mas Capelier F
Orange FS
Mons F
Forcalquier S
Pont du Gard FS
Uzes
Avignon S
Alaunium F
Ste-Anastasie F
Tarn
Nîmes FS
Apt*
Riez FS
Nizza
Nages F
Arles FS*
Entremont FS
louse FS
Aix FS
St-Maximin FS
Béziers
St-Blaise FS
Roquepertuse F
Brignoles FS
Ensérune FS
FS
Marseille FS
Narbonne FS
MEDITERRANEAN
Olbia
SEA

THE ART OF ROMAN GAUL

THE ART OF ROMAN GAUL

a Thousand Years of Celtic Art & Culture

BY

MARCEL POBÉ

PHOTOGRAPHY BY

JEAN ROUBIER

LONDON: THE GALLEY PRESS LTD

Printed in Great Britain by
The Camelot Press Ltd., London and Southampton
for
The Galley Press Ltd
Aldine House · Bedford Street · London
First published in Great Britain 1961

CONTENTS

Foreword, vii
Meeting with Our Past, 1
Hallowed Stones in Holy Places, 7
The Mask, the Head and the Face, 12
Changes in Human Dwellings, 20
Living Waters, 28
Work and Play, 32
Symbolic Power of Animals, 37
Threatened Existence, 44

CAPTIONS

Threshold of History
[Illustrations 1–5]
Art of the Celts and their Predecessors
[Illustrations 6–56]
The Greeks on the Mediterranean Shore
[Illustrations 57–64]
Romanization of Southern Rhône
[Illustrations 65–125]
Rome, a World Power
[Illustrations 126–170]
The New Face of the Celts
[Illustrations 171–225]
Intimations of Christianity
[Illustrations 226–259]

FOREWORD

A THOUSAND years of Celtic culture bring us, in the pages of this book, from the contacts of Greek and barbarian at Massilia (Marseilles) down to Julius Caesar, the conquest of all Gaul, and so forward to the collapse of the Empire: the inroads of Teutonic peoples, and the beginnings of Frankish rule. These things are usually separated from one another in different publications by different authors, and it is often difficult to trace the continuity of settled life and modes of expression that in fact went on, despite invasion and rebellion, century after century to contribute finally to the personality of medieval, even modern, France.

Marcel Pobé and Jean Roubier make a positive contribution in these pages to the widening of horizons. They show the spectacular achievements of Roman power and public administration evidenced for example at Arles, Orange, or Trier, but they show also how native Celtic (Gaulish) artists and craftsmen found new outlets in Roman forms of representation, both for secular and religious purposes, and how these may often amplify the prehistoric archaeological record. At the lower end of the time-scale, we see something of the beginnings of Christian art, and of the organized Church, and these should remind us of the vital part Gaul played in the Fifth Century as a stronghold of Christianity no less than as a centre of Classical learning. It was from Gaul that Christianity came to Britain and Ireland, and the first Churchmen in these islands must be envisaged against the sophistications of Bordeaux and Trier as much as against the wilderness of their chosen mission field.

English readers now have the opportunity to delight in this wonderfully varied collection of fine photographs. The result will be to see the inhabitants of Roman Gaul in much clearer perspective, and to recognize their arts and monuments as part of a continuing heritage in which we may still share. Relevant as is the content to the growth of western civilization in succeeding centuries, there is much that directly concerns, through comparison and contrast, Roman Britain, and its native peoples. Many British tribes had come over from Gaul during the five centuries before Julius Caesar, and many broken communities and individuals were to seek refuge here in the course of his campaigns, and in later troubles. Trade between Roman Gaul and Britain also played its part, and all these links assisted in the propagation of Gaulish ideas and practices amongst the islanders. In this connection it is particularly useful to find in these pages a very representative collection of photographs of sculpture and bronzes to do with Gaulish cult and mythology. It is especially in this field that information from Roman Gaul is most helpful to studies of Romanized native cult in Britain where the material is altogether more scarce. But this Gallo-Roman representative art also illuminates the community of Celtic thought and symbolism over a much greater area for it is very much in accord with the body of information derived from Irish literary sources on the pagan past, and it forms, too, a material body of reference to which can be related monuments, and more rarely inscriptions, throughout the whole range of earlier Celtic expansion: virtually from Ankara to Armagh. Consider the bronze boar with great fringe of spinal bristles from Neuvy-en-Sullias (Pl. 8). He is the most popular beast in Celtic art and story. He was the symbol of plenty, and can be seen identified with this essential duty of a local god, together with the torc, a token of riches, in Pl. 6, or, again, on the battle standards carved on the Arc d'Orange (Pl. 101). In the early third century B.C. another great bronze boar was placed in a Celtic warrior's tomb at Mezek far away in Thrace. In Ireland, the pig played a central rôle in mythological as well as heroic feasting, and those redoubtable animals from the Welsh story of Culhwch and Olwen: Ysgithyrwyn "Chief Boar," and Twrch Trwyth and his seven young pigs, must have been the last of a noble pedigree. The lady seated on a mare, and bearing a tray of fruit (Pl. 181), is Epona, the "Holy Queen" of Alesia, and widely acknowledged in the Celtic world, but in Ireland she appears under different names, such as Macha and Étain, while in Wales, the mare attributes of Rhiannon the "Great Queen" speak for the same cult.

The three Mothers (Pl. 183) bring to mind similar dedications in Roman Britain, but also the triple goddesses of Ireland as in the case of the three Brigits, or perhaps one Brigit three times powerful, and patroness of poets, smiths, and healers. There are many others, and, amongst male deities, insular eyes will look especially at Sucellos (Pl. 172), a very Romanized version this, and compare him with the altogether more robust Irish Dagda who instead of a small hammer struck mightily with his club, and rather than a small jar of plenty, bore about a great cauldron of inexhaustibility. The Esus reliefs from Paris and Trier (Pls. 173 & 174) set many problems in iconography and philology, but sacred trees were also revered by the insular Celts.

These introductory remarks must not end without a word of welcome for the plates devoted to the sculpture from Roquepertuse, and Entremont, in the Bouches-du-Rhône. The subject matter is seen here in any range for the first time in an English publication. This art dates from the third and second centuries B.C., and reveals a rather special state of affairs not typical of the Celtic world in general, but showing the application of Mediterranean art modes to Celtic requirements in an area particularly open to such influence. Quite apart from the impressive seated figures, the iconography illustrates truly Celtic themes in the horse friezes, the sculptured decapitated heads, and in the provision for real ones for display in monumental settings. The groves of Mona destroyed by Suetonius may have witnessed no more barbarous rites than those enacted in these great sanctuaries of the Saluvii.

T. G. E. Powell.

MEETING WITH OUR PAST

ONCE AGAIN, our rambles in the wake of our ancestors had led us in pursuit of their traces off the highway and into the byways. Over the past three decades it had been proved to us over and over again that though history may be faithfully recorded in scholarly writings, it only comes truly alive when we are face to face with visible objects that have been silent witnesses of its events. In order to understand fully the past we must realize it, actualize it, at least in one dimension. This we can do by checking the knowledge acquired in school and libraries at the actual scene. In this way a visit to the oppidum of Ensérune, near to but high above the coastline of the Mediterranean, had literally resurrected the pre-Roman cultures from the Bronze Age onwards, both in the excavations and in the museum; the story being told, now by the explicit pattern of the ruined walls, now by the funerary urns with their grave-furniture displayed in long rows of glass cases. The disturbed ground all round this collection of relics bore witness to the site of their discovery. Shortly afterwards, repeated visits to one of the noblest apartments of the former Augustine Abbey of Toulouse, where for the space of one summer Celtic works of art from all over southern France had been assembled, had provided the opportunity for the most illuminating comparisons. A considerable number of the works exhibited there have been illustrated in this book. Finally, an excursion had led us over the plateau of Millevaches; along its western edge, an upland some three thousand feet high, lie the Gallo-Roman ruins of Les Cars, so disrupted as to be almost unphotographable, with their once imposing baths and the remains of a basilica that must date from early Christian times. This brought the whole range of successive cultures down to the very end of classical times. The harvest seemed so rich that this last expedition might be considered complete.

But still we were faced with the one most difficult question. What had the Celts found in the spacious area later known to the Romans as Gaul, between the Channel and the Mediterranean, the Rhine and the Atlantic, as wave after wave of them wandered in from Central Europe? For they were not the first autochthonous people of this country, watered by four great rivers and innumerable smaller ones, alternately flat and mountainous, still thickly wooded in those days and for the most part temperate in climate. The answer leads us to that crisis of history, or rather of prehistory, when the foreign tribes pressing in from the north-east and the seaborne traders along the southern coast brought the use of bronze, and above all of iron, to the indigenous population whose material and spiritual culture belonged to the vanishing neolithic age. One would almost be led to think that the men of the Stone Age wished to immortalize and do honour to the stone which had served them as the universal tool for thousands of years before it was supplanted by metal, in those monuments which the learned call megaliths—the 'Great Stones,' which have survived into our day.

As chance would have it, thinking such thoughts and musing over the ordnance map, our eye fell on a group of symbols with the legends 'Autel des Druides; Dolmen: Pierre aux Neuf Gradins,' quite close together on the map. The dolmen revealed itself according to our expectations (Pl. 1) after rather more than an hour's walk over somewhat boggy ground; originally the core of a barrow, it stood in the middle of a wood as witness to the earliest attempts of our forefathers at architecture. In pristine condition, unmarred by any later additions or modifications, it lay at the top of a lightly sloping corridor marked out by upright stones, a slab of rock a yard thick, five yards across, resting on seven blocks of differing sizes. It is easy to understand why tradition has endowed such structures with names like the Giants' Table. But the name dolmen is Celtic and means stone table (dol = table, men = stone). For long the megaliths were taken to be the work of the Celts themselves (just as Stonehenge was ascribed to the Druids) which explains this local name 'Autel des Druides.' They are mostly, as in this instance (Pl. 2) sacrificial stones, bearing circular channels with slightly overhanging edges, plainly the work of human hands and tools and not of natural erosion. Between the two hollows there is a high narrow ridge on which the neck of the sacrificial animal rested.

There remained the Stone of the Nine Steps, which we could not find at first (Pl. 3). The landlord of the modest hostelry at Pontarion could only point out approximately the direction of this oddly-named monument. I only relate how we came to find it in order to bring home to the reader the peculiar situation of this monolith here pictured, no doubt, for the first time. Close behind the village of Martineiche there rises on the left a steep slope which the footpath skirts in a wide curve. We glimpsed through the undergrowth, out of which towered oaks of such mighty girth that two men's arms could not span their trunk, the outlines of gigantic stone blocks. The embankment was almost perpendicular and covered with bracken a yard high through which we forced our legs with difficulty. The landlord had indeed warned us that the paths that once led up to the top were very much overgrown. However, we made our way to several blocks of stone, which bore worn but still perceptible marks of tools. After more than two hours we had found two sacrificial stones, but still no trace of the stone with the nine steps. Though we had set out before dawn the warmth of summer began to make itself felt. A stirring in the undergrowth showed that the wild life was waking up. 'What a lot of lizards there are here,' I remarked to my companion. At last we reached the track again, on the other side of the knoll. Luckily a countrywoman came along.

We asked her about the object of our search, telling her of results so far. 'So you've found the Devil's Armchair—le fauteuil du Diable. Those stones were put there by the Druids. Parson said so. Proper heathen things. No one goes there now.' Nevertheless she added, 'The stone with the nine steps is right on the peak of the hill. Some bold chaps have been up there.' Suddenly, she interrupted her discourse, looked at us dispiritedly and declared, 'But you can't walk through the woods in shoes like that; you ought to have boots on. Full of adders it is.' We went no more into the pagan wood that day. But in the following March, while the vipers were still dormant, we climbed past the now leafless trees to the top, strewn with a crown of a dozen blocks of stone. The uppermost of these proved to be the stone with the steps. Hewn out of dark grey granite, a stairway a yard and a half wide leads direct to the summit in the track of the rising sun, and to a view of the whole surrounding countryside. The block had been smoothed off horizontally so that perhaps two dozen men could stand together on it. In the middle of this platform two circular grooves had been hewn, united by a round hole piercing the narrow rim between them.

For us these steps climbing towards the light of day do not signify devils' work, leading as they do to the airy void, any more than all the other megaliths; they are memorials of the earliest age, when the men of the neolithic culture gave evidence of creative art and also of religious thought in the simple heaped barrow and the rough-hewn altar stone, finding its form in the cult of the dead and in gifts offered to a higher being—it may be, even human sacrifice, as the ancient historians tell.

This is the answer to our question. This is the world into which the proto-Celts (according to modern research) and certainly the Celts themselves in the Iron Age, pushed their way with irresistible equipment. This was Europe before the Indo-Europeans. They merged with the autochthonous tribes who had set up the megaliths and in so doing imposed their own ideas on those which preceded them, but not without some change and modification under the influence of the native art, as we can see from the evolution of their decorative themes, traceable through the Hallstatt and La Tène periods. In order to appreciate what that means we must fix our glances on a further development of the megalith, the menhir, which is also an upright stone.

Not only in Britanny with its two layers of Celtic population—the Amorican and the British—are there 'long stones' (men = stone, hir = long). To be sure, nowhere else do they make a stronger and more immediate impression on people of the present day who are seeking to decipher their magic symbols than in such places as the sea-girt peninsula of Quiberon where they present their dark profiles to the advancing waves like ranks of sentinels, or near Carnac, where in their hundreds they populate the desolate heath like a stone procession. Elsewhere they rear up singly at crossroads, as for instance north of the great bend of the Loire, not far from Neuvy-en-Sullias, whence come the most representative bronze figures, both human and animal, that Celtic art has given us (Pl. 47, etc.). Even though these latter only date from the Gallo-Roman period, whereas the menhirs were erected a thousand years earlier and more, despite this disparity of age we were constantly discovering Celtic artifacts in close proximity to megaliths, which may indicate that the Celts and especially their priestly caste and Druids had taken over the cult associated with the megaliths and continued to practise it in some form. In Provence, in the Celto-Ligurian shrines of Roquepertuse and Entremont, the sculptures of which will be treated in some detail below, but also in the Massif Centrale which was thickly settled by the Celts, the same sites yield both menhirs and Celtic artifacts. Even the earliest Celto-Ligurian statues are stone pillars of menhir type (Pl. 25) and the Musée Borely at Marseilles contains a room full of statues from Roquepertuse side by side with menhirs. Just a few years ago—January 1958—a Celtic statue was excavated near Boyouls in Fouergue, exactly in the centre of a circle formed by menhirs. In the same locality more than a dozen hewn stones have been found, showing an oblong form, mostly rounded at the top (Pl. 4 & 5). They are now to be seen partly in the museum at Rodez, capital of the Rouergue, or else in the Musée des Antiquités Nationales at St Germain-en-Laye near Paris. As the term menhir-statues indicates, they are a further development of the menhir in a plastic direction. Here for the first time we are dealing with statues which are not merely, like certain dolmens of individual slabs in passage-graves, adorned with decorative elements such as spiral or stellarform dotted lines and the like, but have unmistakable anthropomorphic traits and must be interpreted as representations of the human form, landmarks in the progress of prehistory.

As our thoughts are progressively freed from the spell of a more or less idealizing realism, and our re-trained eye under the influence of barbaric art and contemporary *avant-garde* European artists we can do justice to these works and their powerful primitive beauty. The figure is totally inscribed on the stone block that stands for the man, his monument, in relief. With all its stylization, the head, the hands with their five fingers, the legs, the feet with their five toes are unmistakable. Characteristic attributes like the important weapons, the sling, sword and belt, are clearly displayed in the centre of the figure. The triangular head, economically sketched in its essential lines only, rounded only at the crown and chin, allows the eyes to protrude by means of deeply engraved outline. The nose is similarly raised from the surface, while the mouth is sharply indicated by a horizontal double groove.

In the study of heads and masks from Celtic and Gallo-Roman sources we must keep constantly before us this first sketch of the human countenance, in order to understand the whole of the subsequent development. A first comparison of the heads on the menhir statues with those of the oldest Celto-Ligurian—perhaps still purely Ligurian—art (cf. Pl. 16, 26, 25) is enough to convince one of that.

In their own art, which brought the legacy of the Eurasian steppe-peoples to the West, the Celts were totally opposed to the realistic—later naturalistic—tendencies of Mediterranean art: one has only to think of their highly ornamented craft-work. Now in Gaul—to give it the name introduced by the Romans—they meet the art of the megalithic culture, developed at latest in the middle Bronze Age, and especially the menhir statues, and this only serves to consolidate their own conceptions. We should not therefore be surprised to find in the high art of Gaul that the influence of the late Classical, Hellenistic or Roman Imperial art of the Meriterranean has been checked, so far as the human form and its portrayal are concerned, by the traditional striving for stylization inherent in the Celts and only strengthened after their immigration; this is true no less of representations of gods like the boar-god of Effignieux (Pl. 6).

So far the human figure in its proper form has hardly begun to grow out of the outline of the stone which is still almost a menhir. Only the head and neck are brought out by lines which are mere sketchwork: on the other hand the neck-ring (torc) is emphasized in relief and given more detailed attention, because of its hieratic significance, than the features themselves. The divinity presented as a man, incorporated with an animal figure, is a transference of Celtic metal statuary into terms of stone carving as is proved by the legs, riveted on even in the stonework, and confirmed by a comparison with the bronze cast of a similar boar (Pl. 7 & 8). In the boar-god of Effigneux we have a clear example of the perfect synthesis, in the sense of domination and slow penetration, of the megalith technique as taken over by the Celts and the metal crafts which they brought with them.

It has therefore not been irrelevant to consider the art that preceded the Celtic immigration, and to display some examples of it. Just as we ourselves are able to enliven our culture by new contacts with bygone cultures, so the Iron-Age Celtic invaders felt the challenge of the autochthonous Bronze-Age sculptures, and, at a longer remove, that of the culture of the late Neolithic, as we can see from its megalithic monuments.

But it must be added at once, that recent discoveries in more northerly parts of Gaul bear witness to a different symbiosis of arts and cultures. In the barrow of a Celtic princess discovered by René Joffroy above Vix in Burgundy there was a massive golden diadem of Celtic provenance round the dead woman's skull, and also a bronze krater or wine-mixing bowl—a sculptured vessel with handles one metre sixty-four centimetres high and weighing 210 kilogrammes—of Greek origin, the largest and so far most perfect example of its kind known to exist. Among the grave goods were not only the parts of a Celtic ceremonial waggon, but also a bowl in Attic pottery and an Etruscan bronze jug. These objects together with others from the same barrow combine to date the burial exactly in the sixth century B.C. The whole find has been mounted in one salon of the museum at Châtillon-sur-Seine.

Study of these remains proves that as early as the end of the first Iron Age (Hallstatt IIb) Celts settled on the upper reaches of the Seine were in contact with the Greco-Italic world and obtained expensive art-objects from it, which have now come to light after two and a half millennia. By a happy chance the authors of this book were busy in the museum with the Gallo-Roman group of mother-goddesses from Vertillum when the giant krater of the princess from Vix was brought in, still covered with clay.

This contact closes the cycle in which the cultures of the Celts coming from the north-east and the Greeks coming from the south-east are united with that of the native neolithic and Bronze-Age peoples, centuries before the entry of the Roman legions on the Gallic scene. To the primitive monuments of megalithic art were added the already highly developed decorative arts of the Celts, soon to be joined however by the more perfect creations of the Hellenistic art of the Mediterranean, brought in from the Greco-Italic area, together with the artifacts of the neighbouring Etruscans which have only recently been assigned their true aesthetic worth.

We should bear this in mind when, five centuries later, the Romans according to their lights speak of the Gauls as barbarians.

HALLOWED STONES IN HOLY PLACES

SINCE THE discoveries at the princely barrow near Vix there has been much discussion among specialists, not only about the source of the foreign grave-gods—that was soon determined—but about the route by which they were transported to Mont Lassois in what is now Burgundy, especially such large and heavy objects as the bronze krater. Was it by the land route: the Alpine passes—the modern Switzerland—the Jura—the Plateau de Langres—or by water: The Mediterranean—the port of Marseilles—the Rhône—the Saône—the Seine? Along both routes both earlier finds like the vase from Grächwil in Switzerland and more recent ones like the Greek pottery of the Rhône valley show that a lively exchange of goods along proper trade routes took place between the Mediterranean and Gaul and even Britain: Britain from which tin, indispensable to the bronze worker, was brought. Archaeology proves again and again the connection between the western Celts and the Greeks. At the same time we have better and better information about the entrepôts.

On Gallic soil itself we are familiar with very important remains of Greek trading posts, on the Mediterranean shore. From Italy to Spain what was called the Road of Herakles led via Nice (Nikaia) and Olbia past Toulon to Ampurias in Catalonia. Among further discoveries of Greek foundations, ports along the mercantile seaway antedating the Celtic immigration, Massalia is the most important, founded by the Phocaean Greeks of Asia Minor about 600 B.C. This was the nucleus of the modern port of Marseilles. There in a ruined shrine of Artemis, who was the tutelary deity of the city as she was of Ephesus in Asia Minor, dozens of steles in the Ionic style were found, representing the goddess seated in the cottage-shaped niche known as a naiskos. We reproduce in PL. 57 the best preserved of these votive gifts which go back to the foundation of the city. The venerable fragment of an Ionian capital from the sixth century, which shows similarity with the capitals of the Artimeseion at Ephesus, and the remains of a town wall built somewhat later, prove that the Greeks of Massalia, where the East-West route meets the North Rhône highway, set up an entrepôt from which commercial relations with the Ligurians could be maintained, but which was also a centre from which cultural influences could be diffused in a peaceful atmosphere, since the Greeks showed no colonizing tendencies and therefore did not seek to subject the inhabitants either militarily or politically. For their part the Ligurians seem to have come to an understanding with the Greek merchants without any friction. For centuries the Ligurians and also the Celts who mingled with them from about the fourth century onwards came down to the Lakydon—as the Vieux Port of Marseilles, which is still in business, was called—to traffic in goods and slaves. It was here that they made their first acquaintance with that convenient invention, coined money, if they had not previously met with it in the course of business with the Phoenicians. Once they had adopted this invention the La Tène Celts took the opportunity to develop their flair for ornamentation in this particular class of metal work, resulting in highly original design and a high degree of numismatic skill.

A Hellenistic stele to Artemis, also found in Marseilles (Pl. 58), either third or second century B.C., shows that the tradition of veneration for the Phocaean Artemis persisted despite all changes of artistic style. A comparison with the archaic stele gives the measure of the long progress, from hieratic severity to almost decadent elegance, of Greek sculpture even at the periphery of its sphere; the static figure of the goddess, completely wrapped up in herself has become a living woman, reaching out sideways with the elasticity of a dancer. It is of the greatest importance to keep this process of the loosening-up of form constantly in view and to take note of what it expresses, which is no less than the humanization of their gods; because the Celts of Gaul, just at this point of time and space, between their own invasion and that of the Romans, were in constant touch with the changing forms of classical art and the religious thought of the Mediterranean peoples: war did little to break this contact. How these contacts with foreign art and religion worked out is shown in the high art of the Celts, either developed in pre-Roman times or actually under Roman rule, of which we give more than forty examples in Pl. 6-56, not counting architectural examples. In the whole of Gaul, but especially in the south and in the lower Rhône valley, an area of great importance for the study of prehistoric cultures in general and their interaction both east and west of the river, Celtic, or more exactly Celto-Ligurian sites have been excavated in which we can recognize not merely settlements or fortifications, but the urban nexus of political, cultural, and above all of religious life: Roquepertuse near Velaux above the valley of the Arc, Entremont above Aix-en-Provence, many hill settlements in the Alpilles, such as Mouries and Glanum above St-Rémy on the northern slope of a range of hills that has been inhabited since prehistoric times, where a hellenistic Glanon has come to light beneath the Roman Glanum and where lately the oldest levels have yielded an autochthonous Celto-Ligurian shrine. It is everywhere noticeable that sites which are originally associated with a religious cult keep their sacred character even as one culture fades into the next, except in cases where they were deliberately destroyed by the Romans precisely because of their religious significance.

In this respect the fact is significant that for instance Entremont was destroyed: for Entremont contained shrines of the gods and heroes of the Salyans—no doubt the people to whom the Romans also referred as Saluvii—which were the centre of a resistance based on religious conviction: when the place was taken in 123 B.C. the fortifications were slighted and the shrines desecrated and wrecked. All the statues excavated there (Pl. 32, 34, 37 *et seq.*, 43, 46) show mutilations of the face and unmistakable traces of decapitation. Similarly at Roquepertuse the statues (Pl. 14, 15, 35, 36) connected with the cult of gods and heroes of the mixed Celto-Ligurian population had been overthrown and smashed. The Romans had been called in by the Greeks who had often been in hard straits since the Celtic immigration began; for the Romans it was simply a question of hitting the enemy where it hurt most, knowing that his dearest aspirations were given visible expressions in these statues. This procedure shows at once the importance of the holy places, whose desecration would deal a deadly blow to the whole corporate life of the tribe and the living religious faith of the Roman invaders who proved by this negative, sterile act of brutality that they believed in the validity of that which they injured.

After the suppression of the Celto-Ligurian rising against Massalia, the driving force of which was to be found in the Celtic warrior element of the inland tribes, the Romans, who had already some twenty-five years earlier liberated Nice and Antibes (Antipolis?) from the Celts who were threatening the Greeks there, built their first important town on Gallic soil, very close to Entremont but no longer on a naturally fortified site, rather in the plain between the rocky hills to the north and the course of the River Arc to the south: it was called Aquae Sextae Salluviorum. Not, indeed, in the much-built-over town of Aix-en-Provence, but in several other towns and cities of Gaul we can point to shrines built by the very same Romans who must have destroyed the shrines of the natives for ideological reasons, containing impressive monuments to their own gods. The Maison Carrée of Nîmes (Pl. 115) founded by Agrippa, stepson of Augustus, and the similar, only better-preserved, temple at Vienne (Pl. 126) dedicated to Augustus and Livia are among the most important of those temples which in Gaul as elsewhere in the Empire attest the excellence of Roman building technique. Both temples allow us to realize what a high priority they enjoyed in the town-planning schedule. As the propagation of the Roman state religion kept pace with the advance of the Roman armies temples sprang up, as for instance the one (Pl. 113) of which clearly visible remains are to be seen on a height between the Via Aurelia and the lower course of the Durance south-west of Vernegues, or the four Corinthian columns with architrave (Pl. 107) at Riey at the confluence of Auvestre and Colostre, in the heart of scarcely accessible hill-country that was once thickly populated with Ligurians.

Although the former Celtic cults persisted under Roman rule in a humanized form, that is to say modified and adulterated, as can be proved from the abundant examples we have illustrated from the Gallo-Roman pantheon, yet we do not know exactly in what way and to what degree the practice of the Roman religion in this province differed from that in the empire at large. P. M. Duval, one of the experts on the mixed Roman-Celtic culture, sums up the matter thus: 'What is to be found in the way of inscriptions and statuary is identical with that one would find in the Roman homeland.' This is borne out by our illustrations of Roman sculpture.

There is an extraordinary wealth of Roman statuary in Gaul that has survived the wars and migrations of two millennia since the days of Roman rule. It is significant that so many of them portray deities in stone or bronze. It will be sufficient to scan the long series of Roman portraits reproduced here (PL. 65–170) in order to meet most of the gods and goddesses who belong to the now universal religious tradition of antiquity and to recognize mythological scenes that have become familiar to us from the world of classical legend. But together with Olympian figures taken over from the Greeks and re-baptized with Latin names like Jupiter, Neptune, Apollo, Mars, Mercury, Venus, Juno, Somnus (PL. 129, 121, 159, 161, 169, 109, 122, 155, 127) we have demigods and heroes like Hercules, Orpheus, Hippolytus (PL. 154, 97, 98) and monsters like the Centaurs, Satyrs, Nymphs and Maenads (PL. 79, 110, 82, 83); even a few oriental divinities brought late in the day by legionaries who had served or even been recruited in the Levant, and mythical beings from the same area, such as the many-headed Abraxas, the Persian Mithras, a Deus Invictus celebrated in mysteries (the sun) who had been preceded in earlier times by the Phrygian Attis, consort of Cybele (PL. 163, 136, 130). The natural corollary of humanized gods is deified emperors, whose worship admittedly was less an act of reverence for the individual ruler than for the institution as such, for the superhuman ruler who was regarded as a being not of common clay, especially in the provinces such as Gaul, even in his own lifetime (PL. 124, 128, 143).

With our present-day Western outlook we find it hard to understand why in this polytheistic empire the provincial inhabitants of, let us say, Gaul, received the first intimation of Christianity as just another of these oriental mystery cults. But whereas the others were capable of being fitted into the existing pantheon—even if some of them like Mithras tend to assume an unusually prominent role—it was soon recognized that the one newcomer differed from all the others in this, that in contrast to the admired temporal might of the Caesars, His kingdom was not of this world, and for that reason His followers suffered persecution, torture and death. His identity was mentioned cryptically by monograms and symbols and this particular way of indicating, and at the same time veiling the identity of the god found a ready echo in Gaul where it was entirely in sympathy with the old druidic traditions of alphabetical symbolism. But when the belief in the One God made man proved itself more potent and more durable than all the mythologies with which the empire had been trying with ever-decreasing success to prop itself up, then the image of Christ began to be openly displayed. Suddenly the tired style of late classicism was convulsed by spiritual energy that people had long ceased to hope for; it did not, indeed, give rise to any new forms but it lent to a dying art its last glamour, and an imperishable dignity to a culture that was doomed to die. We may if we wish regard the sculptures on the outside of the early Christian sarcophagi which represent miraculous episodes from the Old and New Testaments in outmoded terms as only the epigonic expression of a whole world that had not yet discovered the appropriate form in which to express the new content of its thoughts; at the same time we cannot deny that after an era of decadence the holy places are again filled with really hallowed stones. What they have to say to us is as valid and alive today as in Constantine's day, and even the way in which they say it preserves, regardless of almost extinct forms, that aura which cannot be explained on purely aesthetic grounds, that reflection of life, that knowledge of immortality that is already implicit in the heads of Roquepertuse and Entremont as a dark guessing at the truth.

THE MASK, THE HEAD AND THE FACE

WHATEVER definition the ethnologists give to the mask, however they may explain its origin and meaning, they all agree on an artificial face used primevally for ritual purposes. Both at the beginning and at the end of the works of Celtic craftsmanship or in the Celtic tradition described in the first main division of this book, two masks (Pl. 9 and 65) show how the human face was given by means of stylization a form which transcended the single features of the individual and became universally valid though patently based on the living model, thus creating a type. These are genuine masks, that is to say faces modelled out of sheets of brass or bronze, and hollow, though the original dimensions indicate by their smallness that in fact they were not designed to be worn as disguises by living people: for the sake of simplicity we have reproduced some of these masks larger than original. The pipe-like hollow neck of the older mask which belongs to the third century B.C. and to the Pyrrenean area where it was discovered in 1870 shows that it was probably mounted on a wooden shaft and paraded aloft. Raymond Lantier, who was the first to research into the origin of the arts in France and trace them out of prehistory down to the beginning of the Roman occupation, sees in this mask the likeness of a Celtic divinity—'la partie antérieure de sa tête.' It passes our intuition to guess how it was closed at the back (perhaps it was attached to the skull of a child (Tr.)). The manner of stylization is specifically Celtic, not only in the main lines of the faces, enclosed within two curves and browless, in the form and placing of the eye-sockets, in the elongated triangle of the sharp nose, in the linear presentation of the mouth, as also in the fine lines representing the hair which have been treated purely as a decorative pattern; spirals for the coiffure, S-shapes for the beard, fishbone pattern for the eyebrows.

But even the later mask, modelled in the Gallo-Roman period and discovered in 1864 near Chartres, shows typical Celtic features, although it is precisely the comparison of these two objects which demonstrates how in the space of three or four centuries the art of Gaul under Roman influence had evolved in the direction of realism. The brow remains low, with a clearly defined shallow arch over it, marked out by the edge of the swept-back hair; the arch of the brows and the ridge of the nose unite to form two angles enclosing the strongly outlined eye-sockets. The confident interplay of the triangles formed by the point of the nose, the upper lip, the mouth and the chin, gives a drawing which is the classic example of Celtic geometrical art. Further components of the human image as conceived in the traditional Celtic way are the high level at which the ears are set on and the thickness of the neck (though it seems likely that the older of the two masks originally had no ears and its neck was really only a socket for the insertion of a pole).

We should not think of either of these two masks as portraits. They are not meant to represent this man or that man in all his individuality, but, in the earlier instance, a divinity hinted at by a mere sketch of generalized human features, and in the later work, man as such, no longer indeed the outer shell of a supernatural being, but the imposing symbol of aristocratic power. In both masks the representation of the human face is subservient to a ritual purpose which is emphasized by the simplifying, monumental style. Through the picture the tribute of respect is paid to extraordinary power, and its true function is to represent this power. No matter how much reduced or magnified in size, on every scale these works retain their extra-artistic character: their function is hieratic, not aesthetic.

All pre-classical and sub-classical work in Gaul which portrays the human face or form must be regarded in this light and not measured by the standards of representational accuracy which may be valid for other cultures. This is apparent as early as the boar-god image of Effigneux with which we have already dealt (PL. 6) and the god of Bouray (PL. 11 & 12) sitting cross-legged with the feet of a deer and whose left eye still retains an enamel filling of remarkably high quality. Even though these faces are modelled with greater realism they are still dominated by the curves and angles characteristic of Celtic stylization. From the Pyrénées to the Loire and the Seine and the Marne these masks and mask-like busts demonstrate a unity of style which is indeed outwardly modified by contact with Roman art but in principle remains unchanged.

Turning now to the heads of the south-eastern region, the stone statues that have been found at the shrines of Roquepertuse and Entremont, as well as in a wider area on the left and right banks of the lower Rhône, we have to remind ourselves that this is a region only settled by the Celts in the fourth century B.C., before which time contact between the Ligurians, who had been in occupation throughout the Bronze Age and the later Neolithic times, and the seaborne Greek, possibly even Phoenician, merchants, had taken place. We have therefore to deal with two further ingredients that must be assessed in any analysis of the locally developed art which was already quite sophisticated before the Roman invasion.

The oldest three-dimensional portraits from this area are the roughly modelled heads on a sort of stone totem-pole which we show disposed vertically as it originally was, though now it is lying horizontally (PL. 25) in the shrine of Entremont, serving as the threshold of the 'Hall of Heads.' It has been called by the double analogy of 'menhir-stele,' and comprises in all twelve heads, which in the lower tiers are arranged in pairs (one course) and in three (two courses), the central head of the lower trio being reversed. The face is only hinted at by T-shaped markings on the front of the rather long skulls. Fernand Benoit, who has been doing research on these shrines for years past and slowly but with increasing success unravelling their secrets, asks the question: does the absence of the mouth—and indeed of properly drawn eyes—mean death which robs us both of sight and speech? Or have we here some magic means whereby the spirit of the dead man is hindered from breaking out of his dumb and blind image? The very posing of this question presupposes that we are still dealing with 'prehistoric' ways of thought. In the Hall of the Heads, with its pillar-lined walls, was found a further stone (Pl. 26) which poses yet more difficult queries. Side by side with a modelling of heads which is technically of the same order but does indicate the mouth, so that it can refer to someone still living, there are grooves cut in the block into which real raw human skulls were fixed with big nails from which traces of rust are visible and shreds of metal have been recovered; the stone doorposts of Roquepertuse (Pl. 28) also carried skulls. If one calls to mind the passages in which classical authors such as Poseidonius of Rhodes writing of Gaul describe the natives as head-hunters, and takes into account what ethnology can tell us about such practices still lingering among primitive people down to the present day, one cannot escape the conclusion that the head hewn from stone was done with magical intent, put there like a dummy egg in the nest to induce the presence of real heads of flesh and bone in the niches already cut for their reception. Once the real trophy has been brought in, the stone one is chiselled out and replaced by the raw head. Fernand Benoit proposes a more comprehensive explanation in connection with the sign of the snake, symbol of the Underworld, to be found on another threshold (Pl. 27) of the Hall of Heads, which is not at variance with our explanation; according to this, the images of the clan's ancestors and the heads of their slain enemies are united in this 'Shrine of the Spirits' to form one monument to the heroes and the dead. Excavation at Entremont is still in progress. New finds will increase and widen our knowledge of the art connected with the cult of the dead.

Already about two dozen stone blocks, carved with statuary, have been taken from the ruins of the Celto-Ligurian capital which was destroyed by Romans in 123 B.C. They include representations of the human head showing in an almost complete series from earliest to latest a technical evolution which lasted for centuries and progressed from mere scratched outlines to artistically perfect carving, fully in the round. The main types are the simple memorial image in which the head with slit eyes (Pl. 30) or with sightless orbs (Pl. 40) stands out from the stone in ever higher, ever more refined relief. The head found further north, at Montallier in the Alps belongs to this series also (Pl. 16); its plinth, cut away on a slant, bears an inscription not yet deciphered. Beside the galloping horses of the door-jamb from Nages, presumably standing for the Ride of the Dead, two similar heads appear.

Between this and the next group, that is between the mere sketches of the head and the properly sculptured heads, it should be the task of a book consciously written round an ordered series of pictures to point out the way of transition. The double heads of Roquepertuse (Pl. 14 & 15) are first to have genuine charm, coming cleaner out of the surface of the stone, less wrapped in masked anonymity, already on the way to truly plastic presentation. They were once built into a fairly large monument, as we can see from the wedge into which the stone behind the junction of the heads has been hewn. In the fragment still visible from the front between the two heads, we can just recognize the beak of a giant bird which must bear some relation to the bird crowning the door-jamb (Pl. 28) at the same site. In this context the meaning that was attached to the artistic representation of the human is of special importance in this shrine with its skull-adorned doorposts; and above and beyond that the power of pictorial expression that resides in this sculpture, whether it represents gods or deified heroes: in any case they are higher powers, withdrawn and immune from the changes and chances of this life. Both the severe symmetry of profiles and the emphasis on the forehead in both of them denote a workmanlike conception of this difficult subject and a technical competence in stone-carving that is a long way ahead of any of the works we have discussed so far. The form, unmistakably Celtic, has been imposed externally on the block, but from within it is permeated by forces which can only be explained by the continued contact of pre-Celtic population with Mediterranean cultures. The tightly compressed lips, instead of falling into a geometric pattern as in the antique mode which can only produce a mask-mouth, lend themselves here to an expression, a true reflection of a state of mind; instead of the mere ornamental play of line against line they offer a medium for the soul's utterance, of which we become aware when we notice the deliberate dissimilarity of treatment between the two heads, symmetrical but not identical. Their difference is so great that they might well serve to typify the contrast between Life (Pl. 14, right) and Death (Pl. 14, left, and 15). A further conclusion could be drawn from this, that this janus-head typifies both death and the victory over death.

The next group of sculptures consists of work in the round with a hand laid on the top or at the side similar to the figures from Roquepertuse which have a priestly air but perhaps represent gods (Pl. 35 & 36), sitting with their legs under them, bolt upright, and on the other side to the raptorial monster of Noves (Pl. 31) which is also squatting upright, its paws on the crowns of two bearded heads which rest on its hind feet. Detailed comparisons with works of early Greek and Etruscan religious art, but also with similar works from the wide area between the Massif Central, the Rhine, and the Danube result in the conclusion that we have here a ritual gesture of protection, perhaps even of possession, hereby the victory over the power of evil which condemns to death is symbolically portrayed. It is significant that on one of these hands (Pl. 34) a lock of hair that unites the mortal with life is seen hanging down between finger and thumb. The squatting figures of Roquepertuse held in one hand—as is clearly seen in Pl. 36—the thunderbolt associated with Jupiter Taranis, whereas the other hand was laid on a head similar to the isolated heads found at Entremont. The laps of both seated figures are formed into round hollows like sacrificial bowls. But in the case of the monster of Noves we are not confronted with one of these death-conquering gods or deified heroes—like the heroes who in Attic steles lay their hands on a herm—but on the contrary with the triumph of the ravaging power of death itself, with a kind of Cerberus, who devours men both trunk and limbs, but imposes his power on the head. In the double head of Roquepertuse the head on the left with its narrow slit of a mouth expresses subjection to the inexorable power of death, while the head on the right with its living mobile lips, opened as if to speak, typifies the might of the hero who can overcome death.

This attempt at an interpretation brings us to the last group of heads (PL. 37–9 & 43), erected as permanent memorials to the princes, princesses, and military chiefs of the tribes, to living people, by the sculptors who worked at the Celto-Ligurian shrines. We have chosen the best-preserved specimens of these Entremont heads which one and all had been severed from the trunk; despite the mutilation due to the systematic desecration by the Romans, we can recognize in them the high ability of the native artists in the district between the Alps and the southern course of the Rhône in the pre-Roman period. Attempts to trace prototypes in archaic Greek (compare PL. 39 with 57) or Etruscan art—comparison with the oldest heads from Chiusi will suggest themselves—do indeed help to place Celto-Ligurian art in relation to its neighbours, but do nothing to detract from its originality.

Mere imitation is not sufficient to create a style. But this is a style in its own right, as witness the formal relationship between the four heads, which form a unity despite the disparity of rank, age, and sex. The close-set, wide-open eyes, with fully retracted lids, in two instances doubly outlined, under the high-arched brows which are emphasized even in the female head; the steeply sloping angular Celtic nose; the tight-shut mouth, somewhat drawn in, are all most noticeable. The powerful, almost massive chin, rising in a bow-shaped jawline to the well-formed ear; the cheekbone protruding above the flat cheeks; the accurately modelled chevelure growing low down on the forehead, the close-fitting helmet and the splendidly simple female headdress—a wimple falling sheer with strongly veiling effect—hold to the golden mean between a precise realism which only shows the essential lines and a spiritual idealism which expresses masculine strength, a warrior's pride, aristocratic dignity and feminine poise through clear line and the timeless universal language of form. Not only the frontal clarity, especially noticeable in the female head, but also the varied profile aspects and their arresting outlines show a familiarity with the possibilities of the plastic form that can only have been attained through many generations of practice and varied experience. This artist was utterly conversant with the technique of representing the human countenance in stone—in this case a fragile chalk that could only be worked with the greatest care. Simultaneously with the characterization of an ethnic type—the Celto-Ligurian blend—they have bequeathed us the characteristic military and aristocratic attitudes of their tribes' ruling class. Their high art is an abiding witness to their highly developed culture.

This art and this culture alike were destroyed in the last quarter of the first century B.C. by the intervention of the Romans which the Massaliots provoked. At once we ask ourselves: what had the conquerors on their part to bring into the field in the way of artistic activity and cultural values—this field where the autonomy of the Celto-Ligurians had been destroyed by an acquisitive colonialism which had at first been foreign to them? Our selection of pictures allows us to provide the answer in the field of sculpture.

All the more so, since Roman sculpture in contrast to Greek which concentrates on the treatment of the naked body and its gymnastic movements, even in the post-classical era, awards the palm to the draped figure surmounted by the head which is the medium of human expression; indeed, it even prefers pure portraiture as in the bust.

As everywhere where the late flowering of the Republic and the uniform style of the Empire spread with the widening Roman frontiers, we find numerous Hellenistic imitations; for even in Gaul there are many pieces of imitative art which represent a decadence from the Celtic schematic style. Often they are copies of imitative pseudo-Greek 'originals,' only a pale reflection of the beauty that was created in Hellas. Nevertheless, they show how powerfully and at what a long range the Greek sculptors exerted their influence. Under Augustus the tendency to idealization shows a Hellenistic tinge above all in representations of the emperor's head, as in the fragment of relief found at Vienne (Pl. 128) which is caught between individual likeness of portraiture and the symbolization of a generalized ruler-figure. Other of our examples, though, show how despite superficial dependence on Roman traits, the Greeks have given the copies a certain character. Thus the Roman sculptor gives his portraits of the gods a certain seriousness, which instead of gay charm lends a chilling heaviness; it is very evident in the unwrinkled smoothness of marble in the wreathed head of the Venus of Vaison (Pl. 109); it is perceptible as a proud claim to power in the bronze head of an Apollo from Nîmes (Pl. 121); it underlines the personification of Colonia Vienna at Lyon (Pl. 137). Less often a Roman manages to create anew an inherited image, as in our Apollo of Lillebonne (Pl. 161), a splendid piece of bronze work, which is among the treasures of Rouen. The veiled woman's head on a fragment of a Roman sarcophagus from Marseilles (Pl. 92) acts on the sight like a distant memory of the noble features on Attic steles. But it is not from the Greek Massalia, but from Roman Massilia. Where the original charm has been replaced by mere elegance, where beauty is supplanted by fashion, where the failure of inner life leaves an almost visible void, we are able to measure, appalled, the great gulf between the technical perfection and vital abundance of the justly famed masters and their imitators who can only copy a style as hairdressers do (Pl. 122).

Yet it would be mistaken to write off Roman sculpture as mere imitation, nothing but the last chapter of Hellenism. How differently the Roman sculptor works when he abandons marble, which lends itself only too easily to mere slickness of execution, and turns to a native limestone; now the confrontation with different material and unfamiliar technique counteracts the routine of uncreative, continuative tradition, as is always the case with such a world-wide art, bringing the peoples of three continents into contact. The results are works like the little girl's head from Forcalquier with its self-willed mouth (Pl. 111), the unexpectedly lively (at least about the forehead and eyes) masculine portrait from Vienne (Pl. 112) or the head of Hercules from Dijon (Pl. 154) which, backed against a pillar, stands for the supporting power of that demigod just as the slightly bowed head of the boy Somnus from Vienne (Pl. 127) typifies the dream-felicity of the god of sleep.

But Roman sculpture shows its undisputed originality and true creative power in the portrait proper, at the point where detailed rendering of individual features fuse into the plastic figure of a complete personality, so that a masterpiece is born. To explain such an achievement we should understand that the subtle technique of wax casting in death-masks had familiarized the Roman sculpture with all the characteristics of the human face. A head such as that of the magistrate of Massilia (Pl. 94) probably traces back to a wax mask of this kind. The actual connection between funeral masks and portraits is even plainer in the face-helmet found in the burial site at Chassenard and the wrought-iron death-mask of a Roman legionary (Pl. 160). But this custom alone offers no sufficient explanation of the high quality of Roman portraiture. The weak feeling for personality as such, the natural tendency to emphasize one particular feature, the leader-cult, without which the role of the Caesars would be unimaginable, are all characteristic of Roman civilization. Even during the republic successful generals were always trying to seize power for themselves. The portrait of the mighty and of his dependants is therefore a genre to which the Roman sculptor was early accustomed. In the hard bullet head, probably belonging to a kinsman of Augustus (Pl. 123), almost menacing masculinity is expressed but still it remains a general theme. But if one compares it with the head of Trajan, also in the Avignon Museum (Pl. 124), then one really beholds the countenance of the emperor; this is the Spanish-born general who consolidated the frontiers along the Danube and in the desert; this is the ruler, descended from Roman colonists, under whom the empire reached its widest expansion; the reliefs on the column that bears his name in Rome bear pictures of his deeds. The calm with which he mastered his gigantic task, but also the burden he had to bear for twenty long years, resolution and bitterness, speak out of these features. This bust contains the sum of a life and in it one man outlasts the ages.

With their art acquired on great projects, the Roman sculptors in Gaul ventured too on a task at first unsympathetic to them: on the portrayal of indigenous types. Is not the foreign element, derived from the remote province of Spain, to be found in even the features of Trajan? Among our examples there are a dozen heads, in which more or less pronounced Gallic features are evident. Thereby Rome has bequeathed us inestimable treasures, for they show us the likeness of those barbarians from whom we can recognize, across the centuries of migration and conquest and intermarriage, our own Celtic ancestors. We would pick out as the most beautiful example the head of a young Helvetic chieftain (Pl. 145) which shows the precise ethnic type in artistically perfect form. With the aid of the captions other works of the same kind can easily be selected, each in its own way proving the desire of the Romans to absorb the inhabitants of subjected provinces into their ever-broadening world-picture. In the last chapter we shall have to examine the way in which religious faith in early Christian times renewed corporate life and lent to the traditional Roman countenance the nobility of spiritual traits, deifying the human countenance for the last time in a style that was already threatened with extinction. At the conclusion of these remarks which began with consideration of the mask we shall only point to the fact that the mask-form still had its counterpart in Roman creative art. As part of the Greek heritage it persisted in the dramatic masks, in the grinning relaxation of comedy, and in the pitiless destiny-figures of tragedy. We see how it worked itself out in other spheres from the antefixes. Those crown-tiles which knit up the end of a row of curved tiles along the ridge of a roof; the Vindonissa Museum at Brugg in Switzerland has an imposing collection of them (Pl. 200 & 201) in which the ethnic type of the native Gaul appears repeatedly. Roman masks are more powerfully evident in the acroteria that were found among the remains of a mausoleum at Sisteron than proper work in the round. In the ravine which the river Durance has sawn out for itself between the Alps and the Mont de Lure, a *castellum*—Segestero—guarded the northern entry into Romanized Provence. There the winds whistle perpetually through the narrow gulley. Some stone-carver who followed the legions managed to express their essence in over-life-size human heads with pursed mouths and puffed cheeks. The temperate South (Pl. 106), the strong West (Pl. 104); the grim and stormy North (Pl. 105) can be read off from these visages. Especially in the malignant glance of wild Boreas we see how the personified wind can become a figure of myth. Celtic nature-worship and Roman knowledge of mankind have here united to portray the power of nature in this rare and strange work.

CHANGES IN HUMAN DWELLINGS

MOST OF the statuary and mosaics illustrated in this book are no longer to be found on their original sites. Therefore we have to make some mental effort to replace them in their natural setting instead of in the halls of museums, where, it is true, they are sheltered from the destructive onslaught of time, but by this very fact are divorced from their living context. With this end in view we have selected, among the works of architecture, not only the monumental buildings which demonstrate the art and the public life of bygone peoples and states, but also some excavated sites and even some remains of buildings in isolated places which are notable not so much for their aesthetic worth as for the light they throw on the daily life of the ancient peoples. These remains, artistically of modest worth, enable us to answer the question: where and how did the people live whose masks and heads have played the leading part in the foregoing chapter?

Ensérune (Pl. 10), in Languedoc, a site still far too little known which gives the clearest idea of life in pre-Roman Gaul, unites in its dominating position all the advantages which weighed with the pre-Celtic settler in his choice of a home. This is a completely detached, rocky hilltop, steeply sloping on all sides and precipitous on some, rising up more than three hundred feet from a flat, lake-studded landscape between the mouths of the two short rivers Aude and Orb, affording a commanding defensive position. A narrow ridge, easily sealed off by ditches and ramparts, slopes away to the north-west into ponds and swamps which at once deny access to the attacker and afford the inhabitants the chance of a fish diet. Today the railway line and the canal from Béziers in the north-east to Narbonne in the south-west run through tunnels under the eastern outskirts of the rocky little range. Three thousand years ago the sea was little more than six miles away but since then it has been pushed back by the delta of the two rivers. The present road from Marseilles to the Pyrénées still runs along the line of the Road of Heracles—later to become the Roman Via Domitia—that led from the land of the Ligurians, between the lower Rhône and the Alps, to the Iberian territory, which began at the Pyrénées. About midway along it, Ensérune was for a thousand years a staging-point and a guard-house. In Celtic times it developed into an important *oppidum*.

In almost every place where archaeologists have explored Celtic *oppida*—that is, not merely fortified sites without permanent habitation—they came, at the deeper occupation layers, on traces of pre-Celtic settlement. So at Ensérune Neolithic tools, Bronze-Age pottery and a few pieces of hammered bronze with geometric designs and imported metal buttons that could not have been manufactured locally since they are typical of the Hallstatt Celts, have been found.

The remains of hut-like dwellings, partly hewn out of the rock and partly with built-up walls, roofed steeply with branches, indicate too a pre-Celtic population who used open hearths and silo pits. Between the sixth, perhaps even the seventh century B.C., and the fourth, this primitive native culture was permeated by enriching elements of Greek origin such as coins and pottery, partly from Massalia, partly brought direct by the seaborne merchants. Here too we are on the soil of 'Gallia Graeca,' where for instance at near-by Port Vendres remains of Greek buildings have been found.

With the immigration of the Celts there came also the impact of the La Tène (a culture, already highly developed in its way, with a high standard of craftsmanship and an almost industrial level of output, even though the Greeks might call it barbaric), on the already completely fused way of life of the indigenes, materially primitive, with the spiritually and physically advanced Greek civilization. We are specially well informed due to the discovery of hundreds of undisturbed burials with cremation urns and grave furniture as we noted at the beginning of our essay. Hellas, Magna Graecia, Etruria, and the Campania are all represented by artifacts, some of which had been brought a long way. But in metal the creative genius of the immigrant Celts who quickly settled down expresses itself in manifold immutable lines and forms.

But in the remains of settlement, in the cyclopean masonry, which from the fifth century onwards made the height of Ensérune into an impregnable fortress, we see, the influence of the Iberians, spilling over the Pyrénées into south-west Gaul a full century before the Celtic invasion; an influence that lasted through the rest of the Celtic period until the arrival of the Romans and justifies the term Celtiberian, by which the civilization of those times is known over wide areas of what is now France. It is established in the pottery, alongside the Greek and autochthonous patterns, by many pieces of ceramic from beyond the mountains, and also in the typically Iberian weapons, bronze brooches and round cloak-clasps, even in coins and traces of writing.

At Ensérune, which is a genuine hill-fort yet open to intellectual influences from all sides, we can detect a three-way meeting on occupied ground which helps to explain the many-layered culture of south-west Gaul: the classical, that is, Greek, the Italic-Etruscan, the early Roman world, exerts its influence from the seventh century until the advent of the legions: the Iberian world from beyond the Pyrénées breaks in from the fifth century onwards and vanishes only with the establishment of the Provincia: the Celtic world of the La Tène era makes itself felt from the fourth century onwards, so strongly that Hannibal in the third century met only Celts in this area, so stubborn that they resisted the conquering might of the Romans to the end. On this height, early fortified on all fronts, which was not abandoned to the preservation of oblivion until Imperial times, and then in favour of the Roman cities Colonia Julia, Septimana Bitterae (Béziers), and Narbo Martius (Narbonne), there are layers of occupation, which show in the light of excavation to date how the huts of the first inhabitants, equipped in almost cave-dwelling style, developed into rectangular one-roomed masonry houses (as in our picture), arranged in rows, constitute a primitive street, and as they developed according to a plan suitable to the lie of the ground, gave rise to the *oppidum*, a proper town divided into quarters and a typical achievement of the Celt. The increasing population forced bold solutions, the extension of the town plan by terraces along the steep slopes round the high centre.

Throughout the length and breadth of Gaul there are known Celtic settlements, ranging from the temporarily inhabited hill-refuge, only occupied and fortified in time of war, to the permanently inhabited town. Even in the towns of today the *oppidum* with its walls is glimpsed through the modern street-plan, only altered in its externals. A simple example is the elevated nexus of Bourges, between the cathedral and the Palais Jacques-Cœur, commanding the confluence of the Yevra and the Auron: again two water-courses! In Gallo-Roman time the summit was girdled with a town wall, bounding the *oppidum* proper; not until the Middle Ages did Bourges spill down into the valleys on either side, but its centre is still the old Celtic settlement.

The Celtic immigrants for their part had taken over many hill-forts which had been occupied since prehistoric times, and exploited and enlarged the entrenchments that Neolithic garrisons had made. They had a good eye for ground, utilizing every fold and hollow for the tactical exploitation of the terrain. For preference they used high plateaus, if possible with rocky, steeply sloping sides, with narrow approaches and hollow ways up from the plains that could easily be watched. A town like Alesia, minutely described by Caesar in his *Commentaries on the Gallic War* (Everyman's Library, Chap. 69, Book 7) where he gives a brisk and graphic account of the siege and capture, is typical and full of pointers for the archaeologist. But the Roman intervention itself, the whole development of the following two thousand years, as well as natural decay, have all contributed to delete or at any rate wear down the traces of Celtic occupation.

The still largely unexplored (in the archaeological sense) hill country south and north of the lateral road which even in prehistoric times led to the Rhône from the Alps along the deep rift between the Mont de Lure and the watershed of Luberon, belongs to those areas of Gaul in which even pre-Celtic settlements are comparatively numerous and well preserved; on both sides, therefore, of the Via Domitia which was improved by the Romans the route took a course somewhat further south. For about thirty years we have been personally exploring this range elsewhere, extending from the Neolithic through the Gallo-Roman and the Migrations Periods right into the Middle Ages. A very arid, only slowly destructive climate; since Roman times a situation rather remote from the business of the outer world; progressive emigration of large tracts of the population, with a consequent freedom from modern over-building, all these are factors which make the region an inexhaustible vein for the history of art and for archaeology. The very earliest dwellings, still taking the greatest possible advantage of natural formations, show us what kind of buildings the Celts came across in their push to the south from about the fourth century B.C. onwards, but also in what sort of surroundings they settled and with what sort of neighbours they mingled.

It was extremely difficult to show the remains of their houses in pictures, overgrown as they were with vegetation. We must make clear that for demonstration purposes we have been forced to choose examples that cannot actually be shown to be of Celto-Ligurian date except on the grounds of numerous comparisons with unphotographable (that is not pictorially impressive) ruins; they recall the building style of the neolithic herdsmen of the high plateaus that has been dominant in this region for millennia, well down into historic times, unaltered. For the sake of unity we have restricted our choice (Pl. 17–22) to a district in the centre of the explored region which offered the most numerous examples. Let us first briefly describe it: south of Apt, the Colonia Apta Julia of Caesar, there rises a high plateau, an outwork of the Luberon range which is at places 3,400 feet high and 40 miles long, and united to it by the high watershed near Aribeau is a ridge 6¼ miles long and on the average about 2½ miles wide. In the north it dominates the valley of the Cavalon 1,300 feet below it, with steep zigzag cliffs, following the line of the Via Domitia. To the south the deeply-carved valley of the Aiguebrune, a mere gorge in its upper course, offers the only lateral passage through the Luberon range: this river empties into the Durance between Cadenent and Lauris. It is remarkable that near the source of this tributary caves have been found showing traces of prehistoric (Mousterian) occupation. Men have lived on these slopes since palaeolithic times, because the site offered natural protection from enemies.

Our first example of the northerly access to this plateau is a peak, regularly fortified into a strongpoint (Pl. 17) with a flat top difficult of access from which every approach could be observed. Behind it a dry-stone stairway leads from the plateau up to a passage, hewn deeper than the height of man through the rock, at each end of which an easily barred gate marks the summit of a road rising straight up from the valley and paved with stones set vertically. On the plateau to its left there are still traces of a wide road—also stone-paved—which foreshadowing in principle the later Roman technique is raised about three feet above the surrounding ground-level. This is seen from the profile (Pl. 19 & 20). Left and right of the roadway there is a clearly defined kerb, as can be seen on the left of Pl. 19. A crossroads is visible a long way off, due to fishbone bonding in the retaining wall (Pl. 21) which is otherwise laid in a plain horizontal pattern. We have met this style of bonding, or something closely akin to it, not only frequently in this area, but also above the Mediterranean coast near La Ciotat and Le Camp, north of Dijon in the headwaters of the Seine, and on the southern slopes of the Massif Central, that is to say in places which were already settled in pre-Celtic times. But the pattern is entirely consistent with Celtic geometrical feeling.

From Forcalquier on the east to Cabrières in the west (the fullest extent of the Luberon) thousands of round houses have been built, which in many places—as in the plateaus we mention south of Apt—are grouped together as composite settlements of surprising extent. These 'villages,' as they deserve to be called, covering several square kilometres, are ringed by walls sometimes twelve feet thick, strengthened with salient quadrilateral towers at the corners.

The Barruols, father and son, who have taken the study of this region as their province, have assembled valuable data on the position and the hitherto unexpected extent of these villages. They believe them to be the home of the Albici mentioned by Strabo and by Caesar, who calls them 'uncivilized mountaineers, formerly subject to Marseilles' in Book I of his *Civil War*. They have been previously, but wrongly, supposed to have lived on the left bank of the Durance. Be that as it may, we have here a habitation site, partially in first-rate condition, which shows the beginning, as early as Mesolithic times, of a series of building styles practised in civilized countries within the historic period. In the museum of archaeology at Apt and in many little local collections the objects found in, under, and near these stone huts may be seen; they belong to a long era, stretching from the end of the Neolithic to the Gallo-Roman period. The Celto-Ligurian highlanders summoned by Massalia to help them in 49 B.C.—this time against Rome—came from these villages; they were the northern neighbours of the Salyi or Salluvii who lived nearer the sea and from whose shrines at Entremont and Roquepertuse came the sculptured heads with which we have dealt above. Now we ask the reader carefully to compare the round house (PL. 22) with the excavations of the Upper Town at Entremont (PL. 24). It will be noticed at once that despite the disparity in shape—round hut and rectangular house—the actual masonry is in the same unmortared flags.

The seemingly simple construction of the round houses, whose footings are always dug out inside, gives rise to a predetermined form. Above a circular vertical wall, often more than a yard thick, not quite the height of a man on the outside, so that one must bend to pass under the heavy monolithic lintel, rises a conical roof, corbelled in diminishing spirals course by course, as the snow-blocks of the Eskimo igloo are corbelled. As here each stone rests on another and the whole building depends for its very stability on every single component stone, the self-supporting vault is menaced by the displacement of only a few flags. Thus unfortunately only a few round houses have survived, but in these we can see with what truly perfect artistry every course has been made to overlap inwards by only an inch or two the one below it, leaving only the doorway to provide light. Later repairs show up as the merest botching, and modern attempts at replicas can be recognized by their deviation from the original form. These round huts are called Borys or Bories—the word also occurs as a place-name. In the Middle Ages they were called Claparèdes, nowadays they are simply 'cabanons pointus' ('tapering huts'). They have been the subject of much discussion and their antiquity called in question because of the relics left in them by casual squatters in recent times who patched them up and built copies—such occupants as fugitive Huguenots during the Wars of Religion—for instance the round huts standing between Gordes and Sénanque are such imitations, not very true to the model. But we ourselves have excavated from the ruins of a still uninvestigated plateau village objects including numerous stone tools—axes, blades, spear- and arrow-points, together with many type-objects such as sherds of pottery, not thrown on a wheel, decorated by the potter's finger, on which we can clearly distinguish four different types of geometric pattern. Inspection of tools and pottery by an expert from the Musée de l'Homme in Paris allows us to date these things from the Late Neolithic to the Bronze Age. Finds from other sites are Celtic. There are even round huts with associated Gallo-Roman objects. The houses at Entremont have thus an indeterminate *terminus a quo* but a definite *terminus ad quem*, precisely dated by the destruction of the *oppidum* in 123 B.C. That the highlanders at least remained faithful to their style of building in Roman colonial times is a proof in the architectural sphere of the tenacity of Celtic and pre-Celtic formal ideas which break through again and again in native sculpture of the Gallo-Roman era. This is the explanation of a round hut, probably erected by shepherds, over the ruins of the Greek town of Mastramele with its faultlessly fitting squared masonry; but even this hut fails to reproduce the (PL. 59) perfection of the pristine form. We can only tell what the houses at Entremont looked like, arranged in streets, from the remains of the footings which make a ground plan (PL. 24): excavation is still in progress and will probably reveal, besides the neighbourhood that has already come to light, further quarters of the town, principally the Lower Town which lies to the north. These are one-room dwellings, rectangular, with only a few square yards of floor-space, whose party walls served also as supports for the steep roofs. Neatly constructed thresholds with sockets for round wooden door-posts, on which the doors pivoted instead of on hinges; blocks and flags to protect the outer angles of the walls against damage from wagon and chariot hubs; storage cellars containing jars of both imported and native ware; fragments of a simple mosaic; wide streets; sewers, of a sort; thousands of objects arranged and classified in the local museum only just beginning to take shape; all show a Celto-Ligurian population clustering round the tribal shrines on the hilltop, living in a genuine urban community and pursuing a lively traffic and exchange of goods with neighbouring peoples but principally with the Greeks of the near-by coast, which last is confirmed by considerable hoards of coinage. An encircling wall of cyclopean masonry with slightly rounded watchtowers (PL. 23) secured the place from attack, though its elevated position already protected it on its more accessible side from the hinterland.

Despite obvious borrowings from Greek town planning, this Celto-Ligurian *oppidum* (for the use of the Latin technical word is justified) is distinguished from the early Greek city (PL. 60, now identified as Mastramele) just on the west side of the Etang de Berre, especially in the design of the houses; this has been excavated under the experienced direction of Henry Rolland, who calls it 'a classic type of archaic Greek acropolis.' Pottery from Rhodes, of which sherds have been found here, point to the seventh, perhaps even the eighth century B.C. When in the fourth century the Celtic invasion threatened the peaceful exchange of goods with the native Ligurians of the surrounding country—this was at a time when other Celts were sweeping right through Italy—the Greeks had Mastramele fortified with a wall which is so reminiscent of Sicily (PL. 59, 62, 63) that we may assume workmen had been brought over for that purpose from the great island which was then Greek, to protect from robbers the warehouses which depended on the port of Marseilles. Until the downfall of Massaliot sea-power Mastramele formed a centre of radiation for Hellenic culture for the whole lower Rhône region. The city was destroyed in 49 B.C. Centuries later it again gave shelter to the surrounding population against the marauding barbarians during the Migration of Peoples.

After the destruction of the Celto-Ligurian capitals and the subjection of the Salluvii, and after Greek Marseilles had finally ceased to be independent, the way to Roman penetration of Gaul lay open through this important intersection of west-east and north-south roads. Despite the stubborn survival of Celtic ways, the might of Rome which had come to Gaul as a conquering power prevailed even in the sphere of human habitation, by means of intellectual and technical superiority. Even before Caesar's campaigns Roman towns had sprung up in the south. He himself founded some or had them founded; his successors, the long series of Roman emperors, gradually impressed on the whole of Gaul the unified character of the Empire with its world-wide range—have we not recently celebrated the double millenaries of Bâle and Lyon and Grenoble, all founded in the one year after Caesar's death by L. Munatius Plancus? When we now come to consider the examples in our pictures of the Roman passion for building which they communicated to the Gauls, coming from the often impressive but rudimentary settlement of pre-Roman times, we suddenly feel ourselves on familiar ground, between familiar walls. We realize at once that Western civilization, its architecture down to our time, apart from the very latest development of gigantic beehives of flats, derives repeatedly from Roman ways of building and is indebted to them.

The Roman house and the Roman town, as they are preserved at Herculaneum and Pompeii, but are also visible in innumerable excavations, belong to the living heritage of our culture, and the knowledge that we have of them belongs to what we learned at school. When we walk through the remains of single houses and whole quarters of towns at Glanum (PL. 65, etc.) or Vaison-la-Romaine (PL. 108) or under an arch like the Porta Nigra at Trier (PL. 166), we know that they speak to us directly and we need no special description such as the factual descriptive commentary of Rudolf Laur-Belart on the Domus Romana of Augusta Raurica, admirably clear as this is. We remember that the oecus and the cubiculum correspond to our dining-room and bedroom, that the portico and the peristyle are elegant appurtenances that our modern covered ways and interior courts cannot rival in pleasantness and artistry as when the Messii laid out their magnificent house at the foot of the hill at Vasio. Mosaics (PL. 69, 70, 133, 135, 138–40, 142, 146–50) spread their scenes of mythology and hunting, their flowery ornamental borders under the very feet of the visitor, while his gaze wanders over the red-painted walls. The cooking facilities in the culina would not shame any modern kitchen. Baths reached a height of comfort still not rivalled today. Latrines ensured hygiene. In short, gracious living had found its proper setting.

As most of our readers are probably aware, there was an exactly prescribed ritual for founding a Roman town, its ground plan being scored out of the turf by a bronze plough drawn by a white bull and a white cow yoked together. Before our eyes appears the chessboard pattern, of intersecting streets, a network with its principal north-south axis, the Cardo, and its east-west axis, the Decumanus; at both ends of both these stood the four main gates. Overall, this arrangement recalls the layout of the standard military camp (the *castra* of our schooldays) but also owes something to Greek models in the more remote past. We may take the Roman city as the expression of political and social idea, with its roots in a religious conception. The foundations of the city rest on ground that is under divine protection. In the most distant provinces it will remain, though slightly modified, true to the prototype: Rome, the City *A per se*. The meaning of its public buildings becomes clear; round the forum, where the citizens can assemble at the core of the city, are grouped the raised Capitol, the Curiae, important administrative centres, the temples, basilicas, triumphal arches, squares and colonnades—the Capitol being dedicated to the divine trinity of Jupiter, Juno, and Minerva. The house and the city together are the most convincing agents of Romanization.

With all this before our eyes, we can understand why the Celts after initial resistance gave up their huts, half-sunk in the ground and roofed with corbelled stone or brushwood, making a narrow, dark dwelling-place, in order to build houses, villas, and towns on the Roman pattern; why they came down from their hill-top towns into the plain, even though the *oppida* with their high defensible sites and encircling walls represented a certain advance in technique; under the political shelter of the *pax romana* the Celts could enjoy a more comfortable life, offering not only to the townsman but the surrounding countrymen the benefits of superior Mediterranean culture which they had already been tasting in some measure for centuries. We can understand too why they preferred to their own stony roads the mighty Roman *via strata* ('street') along which first marched the armoured legions but after them rolled the wagons laden with the goods of Roman merchants which century after century were to supply the length and breadth of Gaul with all the products of an Empire whose economy embraced the whole of the Western world. No aspect of all the changes the Romans wrought in Gaul is more significant than the transformation of human dwellings and the building of the network of roads that connected them.

LIVING WATERS

JUST AS it would be impossible to imagine the conquering advance of the legions and the acquisitive stretching out of Roman power in Gaul, as everywhere in the antique world, without the incessant and progressive construction of a network of roads, so it is impossible not to take account of the extensive and often new uses to which water was put in the civilization of the provinces subjected to Rome and incorporated into the Empire; the inhabitants of which, called 'barbarians' by the Roman historians, had evolved by example a more fully developed, more truly human existence. In its relation to the liquid element the occupying power which was at first heartily hated began to win the understanding of the Celts to whom springs and water courses, which for the most part still bear Celtic names, were holy forces of nature. The religious custom of offering flowers or sweet wine or some such young animal as a kid (as we read in a narrative ode of Horace) must have seemed quite familiar to the Celts since the problem of water supplies was a grievous one for the inhabitants of hill-top towns, to be solved by the provision of cisterns and tanks for storage but also by sacrifices to procure divine favour.

But it was not until they had learned technique from the Romans that the Gauls had the opportunity of erecting permanent temples in the holy places at the source of streams and rivers. Still in a hollow of the Burgundian table-land, north of Dijon, the foundations are to be seen of a shrine erected in Gallo-Roman times over the source of the Seine and a frequently illustrated bronze statue found there, but not of great artistic value, shows us a goddess upright on a boat, symbol of the Sequana, the navigable river; the bow of the boat is in the form of a duck's head—the typical water bird. A place-name like the Le Val des Nymphes given to a hill above the left bank of the Rhône below Valence is a memory of a spring dedicated to one of the nymphs; this spring is still running today.

The Romans adopted the medicinal springs, in a particular way unknown before their time: there were a large number of such sources in Gaul and the Celts were familiar with the use of many of them. By the building of spas the new masters of the country exploited them for medical purposes. Such place-names as Aigues, Aix or Ax (Aachen) and their derivations go back to the Latin word *aqua* or rather to its accusative plural *aquas*, *ad aquas*. After the fall of Entremont, capital city of the Salluvii, the Romans laid out their new town at the foot of the hill where a warm spring rises and they called their new foundation simultaneously after the water and the victorious consul Sextius: Aquae Sextiae. This name we now have in the form of Aix-en-Provence. In the museum at Chatillon-sur-Seine there is a whole collection of popular *ex-voto* objects, Gallo-Roman dated legs, arms, and other parts of the body which have been found near a medicinal spring. Among the dedicated gifts of this kind we sometimes find plaques and little statues which lend a simple but therefore all the more touching artistic expression to the pious faith of the donor (PL. 220–2).

On the right bank of the Rhône lies Nîmes, called by the Romans Nemausus which is only a latinized form of the name of a Celtic spring-god worshipped at this place. In the gardens which were laid out around this spring there stood several Roman buildings, of which art is still (falsely) known as the Temple of Diana; in fact the remains belong to a Nymphaeum of the first century B.C. (PL. 114). The spring, which was once adequate for the chief village of a Celtic tribe, would not long suffice for the water-consumption of a heavily-populated Roman city, the amphitheatre of which seated twenty thousand. Now Nîmes gives us the opportunity to draw attention to a water-supply system that far exceeded the requirements and the technique of the Celts and is entirely the work of the Romans. After his victories in Egypt Augustus presented his veterans with lands round about Nemausus, which in consequence soon became an important town, heavily fortified and full of monumental buildings (PL. 115, etc.). But it was just at this period of the Empire that the increasingly elaborate public baths were calling for more and more water, so that new supplies had to be laid on.

Thus began the construction of the aqueduct, thirty miles long, bringing the pure potable water of a spring in the neighbourhood of Uzès through a hilly terrain as far as Nîmes. It delivered an estimated twenty thousand cubic metres a day. With an energy which we in modern times cannot match, the Roman engineers overcame natural obstacles and brought the conduit through cuttings and tunnels and over bridges. The greatest of these aqueducts is called the Pont du Gard (PL. 99) still in good shape after nearly two thousand years, though it has had no maintenance since the fall of the Roman Empire. It brought the Uzès-Nîmes water-main across the deep valley of the Gardon. Built on completely functional lines for a purely utilitarian purpose, it is an astonishing work of art which the architect seems to have achieved in spite of himself. Yet its beauty is specifically due to the happy proportions of the three tiers, the number of pillars and arches in which were not determined by simple mathematical progression, but varied in their height, length, and breadth so as to fit the contours of the ground. Thus the arch which actually spans the bed of the river at its lowest level has a wider spread than the others in its lower and middle stories, while the third story which actually carries the conduit consists of four instead of three arches over the midmost lower arch. The aqueduct as a whole is not drawn in a straight line from bank to bank, but is slightly curved, the better to offer resistance to the wind. On the faces of the piers some stones were deliberately left 'standing proud' to afford a footing for scaffolding poles and were later used in the maintenance of the fabric. At the point where the arches begin to spring there are sills which originally supported the wooden templates which supported the arches until they were locked with a keystone. Beauty and utility are thus united in this Roman work carrying water over water.

Though partly decayed, the smaller aqueduct of Barbegal (Pl. 88), which similarly brings the water from the Alpilles to the town of Arles on the banks of the Rhône, demonstrates the manner in which the actual conduit of solid masonry was roofed with thick slabs and lined throughout with cement. The same deities which presided over the springs also patronized the aqueducts which served them, as we see from the votive altar hewn out of the rock east of Fontvielle, with a mussel-shell design and an inscription linking the altar with the Barbegal aqueduct. Further south one arm of this double system cuts straight through a hill that rises up from the plain and falls quite steeply on the other side, by means of a channel smoothly hewn from the rock. This sharply sloping channel or water-ladder was used in later Gallo-Roman times to drive a battery of water-mills, sixteen in all echeloned down the hillside (Pl. 89), so that the same water from one central leat served all the mill-wheels.

Naturally the Romans, even in Gaul with its many streams and rivers, needed waterways, so far as these were navigable, for the transport of goods. In the lapidarium of Avignon a relief (Pl. 210, 211) from Cabrières d'Aygues (the second element of this name means 'water') shows barges on the Rhône laden with tuns and drawn along the river by gangs of boatmen hauling on the tow-ropes. The still more famous barges of the Moselle in north-east Gaul are to be seen in the provincial museum at Trier, giving a lively picture of Gallo-Roman civilization on the left bank of the Rhine (Pl. 212–13). In the same museum there is a relief showing side by side the chief means of goods traffic side by side—the wagon and the sailing barge.

Wherever the Roman roads came to a river, or even a stream, they built bridges, some of which have so stoutly withstood the passage of time that they are still in use in our days. As for example below Apt, Caesar's Colonia Apta Julia, where we have the bridge over the River Calavon, with its piers pierced through the upper part so as to lessen the pressure of flood water (Pl. 90) and likewise the elegant little bridge over the Encreme (Pl. 91) near Cereste which has admittedly been restored but is still essentially the Roman structure of piers and arches, carrying the Via Domitia, which can still be traced here and there, from the Alps westwards.

Consecration of the spring, purposeful exploitation of its waters—who can fail to commend the Romans? Towards the end of the first century B.C., Agrippa had the Nymphaeum of Glanum renovated; it had been, as H. Rolland, in charge of excavations, has demonstrated, enlarged in Hellenistic times, with steps leading down to it (Pl. 71). But the son-in-law of Augustus who represented the imperial authority in Gaul was not content with this. He also commanded a small temple to be built over the spring which he dedicated to Valetudo-Health. It is the positive contribution of the Romans that they furthered the hygienic welfare of the population by the lavish provision of water in their cities; the grandiose sewage systems, traces of which can be found all along the streets in such places as Vaison-la-Romaine, assured sanitation; public baths and latrines also raised the general level of health. The hypocaust systems of central heating, as in Pl. 73, command our unbounded admiration, utilizing not only the fire but the gases it gave off, and providing not only space-heating with warm air but also the means of heating water for the caldarium, the 'Turkish' bath as we would call it.

But what began as a salutary care of the body became with time an excuse for unhealthy luxury. It is noticeable that the space allotted to baths in town planning tends to get larger and larger. When we consider the later public baths, such as the finely rounded apse which forms only a part of the baths at Arles (Pl. 87), or the inner room, imposing in its height and width, of the splendidly vaulted hall of the baths of Lutetia still preserved in the heart of Paris (Pl. 158), or even the ruins of the imperial baths at Trier which still form the remnants of a magnificent bath-place, then even we with our twentieth-century ideas of comfort must have second thoughts. We know indeed that the Roman devoted an ever-increasing portion of his day to the cult of the body. We read in Seneca and Juvenal of the critical and satirical attitude taken up towards these habits, which were even castigated as harmful vices: 'Six hundred thousand sesterces are being spent on baths,' reports one of them. 'A man nowadays thinks himself poor and underprivileged if he has no bathroom with expensive marble walls,' says the other. And we understand that at last a stage has been reached where the bathing system no longer serves a hygienic purpose and thus represents social progress, but is the outward sign of a profligate luxury, a symptom of the decadence that is to destroy the Roman Empire.

For all that the waters continue to flow. But meanwhile there are new hordes of barbarians on the frontiers: they are innocent as yet of bath-salts and soap and they batter at the ramparts with all the vigour of a people on the move, whom detergents will not deter. Still in the sheltered inner provinces a doctrine has made its way via Rome from the East, despite the bitterest persecution, into the well-watered valleys of Gaul, And this doctrine, spreading without pause, also speaks the language of water, but in quite a new way. The fish, which formed a charming border-design to the oldest Gallic mosaics, the centre of which was filled by a net (Pl. 69 & 70), now breaks the surface again with new meaning as a divine symbol (Pl. 254). A mysterious fisherman appears as the partner of the Good Shepherd (Pl. 228). We have the miracle of the loaves and fishes (Pl. 243). And history itself now witnesses a miracle; the gospel of the weak overcomes the empire of the strong. On the outer walls of the sarcophagi which still preserve their classical form appears a Hebraic figure who strikes the rock with his staff so that a stream of living water bursts from it (Pl. 234 & 242). This miracle-worker, identified by some with Moses, is in fact Peter 'the Man of the Rock,' of whom we read in Acts 10, journeying to the house of Cornelius at Caesaraea to baptize that centurion and so begin the world-wide Christian mission to the heathen. Just before Gallo-Roman civilization was flooded by the waves of Germanic invaders the octagonal baptisteries in Roman pillared style begin to arise, with a sunken font in the middle where the living waters of baptism were to bathe not only the bodies but also the souls of men, bringing them salvation (Pl. 251).

WORK AND PLAY

IF THE men of whose art and culture we treat here, that is, the mixed population of Celts and earlier inhabitants in Gaul when it was conquered and occupied by the Romans, were constantly turning their regard from this world to the next, if their existence was subjected to higher powers both by the natural order of things and by political and social causes, and if in the end their conversion to Christianity only bound them the more closely to the supernatural, we should not be blind to the fact that they also brought their material existence to a high level of cultivation during the period under review. They progressed from prehistoric conditions under the influence of enriching drafts of new blood and borrowings from neighbouring civilizations that penetrated peacefully, especially in the sphere of art. Of the three important exhibitions which, while this book was being written, brought Gallic artistic achievements clearly to the notice of the modern educated public—Paris 1955, Toulouse 1956, and Schaffhausen 1957—the last above all went beyond mere aesthetic display to demonstrate the connection of art with the entire culture, as was meaningfully expressed in the 'documents' on view. There in the All-Saints Museum were conjured up the astonishing craftsmanship of the Celts, their skill in animal husbandry which classical authors praised, their highly developed industrial activity, as in tanning and saddlery and blacksmith's work (they it was who brought iron into Western Europe), their far-flung commercial relations facilitated by the fact that they minted their own coinage.

One cannot but be struck by the absence of scenes from daily life, both in their original fine arts, in their sculpture before it had been influenced by the Romans, and in such native art as persisted 'underground' in the Roman period. Gods, demons, heroes, princes, princesses, priests and warriors were fitting models for their artists, but never a tradesman or a farmer or a merchant; these might 'sit' for tombstones (Pl. 30, 40) but never for statues.

Among the sculpture of wholly Celtic inspiration, the bronze statuettes from the hoard at Neuvy-en-Sullias in the heart of Gaul, and similar sites that have withstood the passage of time, representations of the human form, show us a class standing midway between the two groups mentioned above, the artists—not the sculptors themselves but dancers, male and female, jongleurs, minstrels and musicians. But from all we know of the Celts themselves and their attitude to life, these are not entertainers in the popular sense, but sacred performers, who practise their art at seasonal festivals as part of religious cults. They are doubly significant for our knowledge of Gallic culture at that time; both in content and in form.

The literary remains which have come down to us in the shape of the old Irish verse concerning the Celtic cycle of quarterly religious feast-days are illustrated for us visually by these little bronze figures arrested in the midst of ritual gestures. In the second volume of his comprehensive history of the Celts, H. Hubert says of such texts that these feasts were primarily religious assemblies, saturated with myth and legend. The festivities included horse-races and races for women. The two female figures (PL. 47 & 51) but especially the second, in which from the rear a sprinting attitude of the legs is easily recognized, shows in ritual nakedness such as we see in statues of the gods (PL. 190) either a dance step or the act of running. We have also two nude male figures, a dancer (PL. 48) whose supple joints betray a swinging rhythm which is also evident in the bowing of the head, the opening of the mouth, and the slightly ecstatic, far-away expression, and a jongleur (PL. 49) whose activity can be guessed from the position of his hands and the attitude of his head, besides the folded napkin on his forehead, in the folds of which the ball will be caught. The man we take to be a musician has on a check jerkin and breeches; once he held some instruments in his outstretched hands. These pieces, not made until Gallo-Roman times but hidden away from profane robbers in a secret cache, demonstrate that the Celts of Gaul must have learnt from the Mediterranean peoples something of classical art and in particular the Hellenistic love of the moving figure, and have learnt to model in the round. Yet the idiom of their form is not a mere subservient copying but an independent treatment of the figure, capable of so fixing gestures in metal with a characteristic consistent urge to stylization, that the movement has all the charm of an instantaneous photograph, but yet has far greater significance than that of a momentary glimpse. It is a supreme example of artistic sublimation, almost distortion, in the service of ritual needs, applied to the female figure through a deliberate heightening of stature and a splendid extended posture of the arms whereby mere naturalistic imitation gives place to veneration.

Such an effect is not achieved merely through exaggerated slenderness but can result from other, no less impressive, measures of stylization; witness the small but truly monumental figure of the god from Mandeure, which was once gilt (PL. 56) but is now only bronze. Niklaus Duerr is preparing a monograph on this. The right hand, resting on a vanished shield, and the left, which probably once held a staff, combine to form a double sideways movement of the arms which lend the massive throned warrior—Mars or Mercury—a strength which broadens the torso and with its gesture of laying aside a weight provides powerful support for the majestic, almost threatening posture of the head. The gathered seam of the cloak, slanting diagonally across the figure, is one of the most exciting achievements of Celtic style, making itself felt in spite of Roman influence. We would draw the attention of the reader to the way in which, with all this group of figures, the varying opening or clenching of the hands is exploited, the crooking or spreading of the fingers, the wide angle of the opposed thumb, lend life to the whole body, while from figure to figure the expressions of the faces bring variety to the pervading seriousness of the game, and in the case of the bronze figure last mentioned the ruling status of the god is emphasized, in whose honour these games were celebrated.

Although the Roman sports also go back to religious festivals and have their roots in the ritual of funeral games, yet as portrayed in Gallo-Roman art they are wholly secular, degraded into mere entertainment, to break the monotony of workaday life. On the other hand work itself, the daily professional activity of men, is endued with grave solemnity whenever Roman art attempts to perpetuate the life of mortal men as a memorial to the dead. The funeral stele of the Roman Empire, anywhere, decorated with figures, aims to perpetuate daily life. These reliefs preserve for the survivors the deceased in his characteristic habit as he lived. Say he was a clogmaker, then he will be shown in his workshop, surrounded by the tools of his trade (Pl. 214); or a well-known clothier, so he is shown in his favourite attitude, spreading out a piece of cloth for the customer (Pl. 215). In similar wise we have pictures of payment of rent or taxes, in which the bearded, hooded peasants are clearly distinguished from the clean-shaven *publicanus* (Pl. 216). We see how the confectioner exposes his round cakes for sale on his stall, while the customer points with two fingers to the delicacy he fancies (Pl. 217). Or at the solemn Feast of the Dead we witness the children at their meal, not forgetting the dog whose little owner is threatening him with a stick, while a boy plays the flute and an elder sister, standing up, supervises the table manners of her little brother (Pl. 218). This last scene, a variation on a popular gravestone theme, is specially worthy of notice on account of its asymmetrical and yet harmonious division of space.

So death is above all an excuse for the picturing of life, the daily life of Gallic provincials under the Empire. But certain events typical of the Empire, customs derived from Celtic tradition, the penetration of Roman culture to the conservative rural masses, and a hundred individual traits by which we can pick out the manners of those times, are also to be found in the other works of art reproduced here. We would only point to the domestic activities of women, simply but unforgettably depicted in the three figures of the Matronae (Pl. 183), one of whom has her knees crossed—a symbol of distinction—and holds the baby in her lap; the second has spread out the swaddling clothes while the third holds the sponge and the bowl of water ready to give it a bath. How often have historians pointed the finger of scorn at the Romans for their evil institution of slavery, as if this subjection of man to more powerful man had not happened in all ages and in all regions of the earth, and in slightly altered form were not still practised today. But Gaul, where before the times of Marius and Caesar the Celts themselves kept slaves, was the province where, under the *pax romana*, the noble custom of manumission flourished. A stele from Avignon (Pl. 84) commemorates one of these magnanimous gestures: mistress and free woman share the same memorial, and the intertwining of their hands and of their looks unite the two women—she who gives and she who receives. Note the patrician charm of the beringed fingers putting aside the veil.

Life in a villa, one of the numerous estates all over Gaul, sometimes quite luxurious, which in our day are exciting more and more the emulation of archaeologists, would show how husbandry, already quite highly developed by the Celts themselves, was improved by the Romans, and how the peasant—the *agricola*, that hard-worked masculine in- *a* of our first Latin book—also derived benefits from Roman civilization. This is much more vividly seen in a mural, now in the provincial museum at Trier (Pl. 167) than in the mere stumps of the actual walls of Gallo-Roman farmsteads which can only be effectively photographed from the air. The Romans with their utilitarian bias valued relaxation as a stimulus to further work. But also the Imperial government set great store by the periodical assembly of provincial townsmen together with the farmers of the surrounding countryside, and for this purpose provided the now famous 'panem et circenses.' Gallia was pre-eminently a corn-producing province. And those who produced the bread must be stimulated by games. What these games were like can be seen from our pictures of sport and stage under the Romans, which show the circus, the theatre, and the amphitheatre in all their technical efficiency, their gigantic scale and their lavish equipment.

The scenery with the vanishing 'curtain' (it went down instead of up as in our theatre) is preserved at Arles, in front of the semicircular rows of seating (Pl. 77). These seats, often dug out of a hillside, were faced by an enormous proscenium, typical of the Roman theatre, as at Orange, where in the upper part of the walls the projecting stones, called 'ravens,' may still be seen, on which rested poles supporting the awning or velum (Pl. 100). We have deliberately shown rather a large number of the very varied designs with which the interior walls of the theatre with its pillars and reliefs were enriched. For it is in this sphere that the Roman architectural *forte* lies; sculpture is made subsidiary and ancillary to architecture. Pillars with architraves give the walls an articulated effect through the interplay of the horizontal and the perpendicular (Pl. 78). Life-size reliefs of Nikes and Maenads (Pl. 81–3), friezes of centaurs (Pl. 79), cupids driving chariots on a smaller scale (Pl. 80), still smaller but yet plainly visible animals in such positions as the proscenium on what was called the pulpitum, all combined to add a festive effect (Pl. 131, 132, 134). All 'grand' styles are at their best in the decoration of public buildings.

The amphitheatres, which at Arles (Pl. 85, 86) and Nîmes (Pl. 116, 117) are in a remarkably good state, illustrate exactly what an expert in architectural history, Nikolaus Pevsner, meant when he wrote that the arches and vaults of such mighty proportions as are found in the Roman aqueducts, baths, theatres, palaces, and basilicas or public assembly rooms excel, from a purely technical viewpoint, everything that the Greeks produced. This they do by their internal stairways and corridors, as well as by what is left of their decorative friezes. Pevsner sees in these buildings, among which the amphitheatre represents the peak of the colossal style of architecture, creations of the Roman feeling for power. A power that rested on the favour of the people.

That is why, relying on the broadest popular basis, the authorities gratified the mass desire for spectacle in the circus. It played the part which our modern sports stadia on the outskirts of cities play now. That racecourses are even portrayed in mosaics shows how popular they were (Pl. 140). Our detail shows a race in progress, together with the palm branch and the laurel wreath which formed the prizes carried by youths, to be awarded at the close of the meeting. St Paul in one of his Epistles has a metaphor of earthly reward in terms of the athlete striving in the stadium, to symbolize the unwithering crown of spiritual victory, thus showing what a powerful hold these spectacles had on the popular imagination in the Roman Empire.

SYMBOLIC POWER OF ANIMALS

Another time I was enchanted.
I was a kingfisher, I was a young salmon
I was a hound, I was a hind,
I was a buck upon the mountain.
I was a butt, I was a spade,
I was a hatchet in the hand.
I was a light speckled cock
Treading the cackling hens.
I was a stallion of a stud,
I was the bull of a farmstead.
I was a grain in the furrow's womb;
I grew up on the hill.

TALIESIN.

This sort of passage often occurs in the old Welsh laments and magic lays of the heroes. Long after their first contact with the Romans and after they had adopted Christianity, the Celts of Britain, threatened by the invasion of the Angles and Saxons, wrote down the legends and poems of their pagan ancestors to preserve them from the newcomers. Into this written literature went, along with later classical and biblical accretions, much of their original heritage. Thus in a lament appears the bard, singing of his dead patron, with the dead man's head: 'I hold in my hand the head of him who was a noble eagle'—in strophe after strophe this head is apostrophized; or again, among the deeds of which Uther Pendragon boasts, the most significant runs: 'Have I not smitten off a hundred heads?' And at once we remember what the ancient authors said about the Celtic head-hunters; we see again the heads of Entremont and Roquepertuse and from such texts we understand their meaning. But the dominant motif of these Celtic songs is the magic of nature which surrounds and masters man. Forests, rivers, mountains, valleys, become living beings, and the animals appear interwoven with them, now as the quarry of the hunt, now as a poetic simile in honour of the hero, but more often as the final stage in a mysterious chain of shape-changes, not in the sense of mythological metamorphoses, as the Greeks so clearly conceived them, but mysteriously, as they appear in folk-tales today. Admittedly the Greek fables and the Celtic stories go back to a common oriental source, but that which is sharply revealed in the light of the bright Mediterranean sun over the islands of Hellas and its shores remains for ever in the dark after the endless wandering over the wide steppes and the gloomy forests.

This magical mixing of beings, regarding gods and heroes as men who have turned into beasts, assumes concrete expression in the boar-god of Effigneux (Pl. 6) or is hinted at in the beast's feet of the squatting god at Bouray (Pl. 11). But since among the Celts figure sculpture, fundamentally opposed to their natural bent for geometrical abstractions, does not occur until after contact with the Mediterranean peoples and their realistic representational art, their conception of the animal god has come down to us mainly in a transposed form.

In the lament of Llywarch Hen for Geraint son of Erbin, the horses of the dead man are conjured up in repetitive strophes of magical alliteration and assonance with fantastic chromatic variations. The frieze of Roquepertuse (Pl. 13) which is actually a fragment of a doorpost from the shrine, comprises a row of horses' heads, one behind the other, as it were in a procession; they are little more than sketches in relief but marvellously impressive in the drawing; the head at the end on the right is full-face, and thus emerges from the magic repetition into the sphere of realism. In the frieze of Nages two death's-heads alternate with two galloping horses seen in profile (Pl. 29). Scarcely visible, because only scratched in, is the decoration of similar horses in motion on the plinth of a warrior's bust from St Anastasie (Pl. 41). In the Gallo-Roman period there appear animal figures in the round, of which we reproduce some here: the boar and the stag from Neuvy-en-Sullias (Pl. 8 & 54), as well as a horse found elsewhere (Pl. 53) and the head of a bull (Pl. 52), with rebated horns which must therefore be a domesticated and not a wild animal, if not actually a tame (performing?) one. Celtic stylization still predominates in these four sculptures, and indeed until quite late in the Roman period animal portraiture is the sphere in which Celtic influence best conserves its strength and native character, as shown in the mane of the horse and the typically ornamental treatment of the deer's coat. Statuettes of animals, found in Helvetic territory, in Switzerland (Pl. 194 & 195), though they depend to a certain extent on Roman models, show Celtic treatment in the heaviness of hoofs and paws, symbolizing their earth-bound nature. Not only in the actual drawing, but in the primitive, quite un-Roman technique of the carving, Celtic style is preserved in the unique animal fragment from Vindonissa (Pl. 192), apparently the head of a hunted hind. The carving in a Hellenistic frame, from south-east Gaul, is an example of Celtic content in Roman form; besides the cock which is a Latin pun for 'Gaul' (gallus) there appears in it a boar, an animal sacred to the Gauls, though this one is not wild but a male domestic pig (Pl. 193). The same animal stands, in an attitude that still owes much to native ideas, on a standard flanked by Celtic shields found in a carving on the south coast of Gaul. It is rotund but rather leggy, therefore perhaps wild and not a porker (Pl. 188). Note the typically Celtic stylization of the hackles in Pl. 193. The almost enforced stylization of the mane is shown clearly in Pl. 189, the head of a pony which was either a votive offering or a toy from Eysses.

Up to now we have dealt only with the native fauna, either wild or domestic, among the latter especially the horse (or rather pony) which played such an important part in Celtic life, either in harness or under saddle. But with the approach and finally with the penetration of the classical Mediterranean cultures foreign animals, seeming exotic to the Gauls, appear on the scene, principally the lion which derives as an artistic motif from the Near East; familiar to the highly developed civilizations of Mesopotamia, it recurs again and again in antiquity, as a figure in mythological scenes. We have one archaic, pre-classical picture of this predator in the Lion of Arcoule (PL. 64) which was found near Les Baux but is kept at Arles; it must surely be the strangest example of a synthesis of oriental subject (brought via Greece) with Celtic traits in the execution of the carving, especially in the treatment of the eyes. Whether and if so how far this archaic lion served as a model for the rather vague monster of Noves (PL. 31) cannot be accurately assessed, and we present it more as a subject for discussion. It has been called a wolf and also a bear, but the latter is very unlikely.

The lion, so familiar to us in classical sculpture, appears often in Gaul, as for example the leonine heads in combination with plant ornament and wearing an almost human expression from Glanum (PL. 74); the lion bust of Vertillium, now at Dijon (PL. 151) with its mighty mane, and the complete figures of lions from the decorative frieze in the Vienne theatre (PL. 134). This frieze forms what is called the Attica, the upper part under the cornice of the pulpitum; it ran along below the stage the whole length of the orchestra, drawing the attention of all eyes to it. The material of this ornamental carving is Carrara marble, and the pseudo-archaic form of the lions makes us think, as Jules Formigé in his study of the theatre at Vienne has ably demonstrated, that it is the work of Greek carvers, who fabricated such figures in or near the actual quarries of Carrara. We are fortunate in that the archaeologist was able to reconstruct this animal frieze in its entirety from the remaining fragments during the restoration of the building and terraces on the site, thus showing the carving in its proper setting. The lion holds pride of place in the centre of a group of stallions, bulls, he-goats, leopards (PL. 131), and dogs (PL. 132); that is to say in company with animals significant for their association with Dionysos, as game and as sacrificial beasts; as such they are frequently seen in Gallo-Roman mosaics (PL. 135 & 139). We have therefore prefaced them with the handsome shepherd Attis (PL. 130) with whom Cybele, who is often escorted by lions, fell in love, and who made him her priest; in the midst of them is seen Orpheus, able to tame the wildest of them with his music (PL. 133). The series ends with the animal torso entwined with serpents, part of the entourage of Mithras; unfortunately the leonine head has been broken off, but the trunk is still quite recognizable (PL. 136). This whole group is significant in the evolution of art, uniting as it does three continents in the Roman Empire, that ever-expanding political unit in which the birds and beasts of Africa and Asia were brought by means of realistic art before the eyes of west-European people for the first time in the historical era.

In such art as the Romans brought to Gaul the horse, long familiar to the Celts, figures mostly in close association with man, not like the unsaddled totem god Rubiodos which was worshipped at Neuvy-en-Sullias. We see it as a charger and as a hunter (PL. 96, 98, 164); as a draft animal in the service of man, either for sport or for transport; even as the object of commerce (PL. 207), brought to the fair by a horse-dealer, valuable enough to be cared for by the veterinary surgeon (PL. 206). But the gods too used this, the noblest of the beasts tamed by man, both under saddle and in harness for their celestial journeys, and nowhere is this more beautifully portrayed than in the great mosaic of the gods from Boscéaz (PL. 146–50), where in the Olympic circus scenes the half-human, half-animal spirits remind the Celt of his own world of fable.

Animal beauty is splendidly exploited in its movement by many carvings of the hunt, which show in detail how hares were netted, and stags too (PL. 86 & 191). The massive but compact bulk of the bull of Rouen (PL. 162) is a demonstration of how to express the essence of the beast in the round, where the realistic suggestive power of Roman sculpture is sufficient to make a single specimen the valid representative of a whole species. Anatomical accuracy is the keynote of the amphitheatre decorations (PL. 118, 119). Inevitably the eagle, the mascot-image of the Roman legions, is frequently represented (PL. 120, 152). The old she-wolf suckling Romulus and Remus goes back to the foundation of Rome, a legend perpetuated in the carving from Aventicum, where the old foster-mother stands protectively over the twins. This is realistic: bitches, vixens, and wolves nurse their young in this attitude (PL. 141). In general, the whole corpus of classical legend is full of animals. In the acroteria on either side of a gable on a pagan sarcophagus (PL. 95) we see Oedipus and the Sphinx on the right and on the left a scene from the *Odyssey*. The nurse will not be satisfied until she has seen the scar on the man who claims to have grown up into the king of Ithaca and was once her fosterling; but the faithful old hound rolls at his feet to welcome him home, joyfully wagging his ears in recognition of his master —an unforgettable example of Greek *dualis*! Besides such almost human traits, familiar to us from Greek poetry, the daemonic character of other monsters, imported into the Roman Empire from the Orient, repels us; such are the curly-tailed abraxus (PL. 163), a bird-god or god-bird, of which we have a small bronze example, found on Helvetic soil.

Although the beasts figure in the classical art of the Gallic region, on the one hand in the company of gods and heroes as the animal personifications of the Graeco-Roman world of legend, and on the other hand as proof of the richness and complexity of practical life after the process of romanization was complete—hunting, trade, farming, transport, veterinary science—they also survive after the rationalists had tried to explain the Celtic gods neatly away, constructing out of the intelligence reports which the legions rendered on this subject a complete equation between the Gallic and the Roman pantheons. A neat but unsuccessful enterprise. To be convinced of its failure, one need only look at the divine couple from Lutetia, obviously modelled under Roman influence (PL. 169–70), and then at the dozen Gallic deities who here are represented by only a small selection from the realm of nature, thickly populated with Celtic godlings who are only personified weather, etc. (PL. 171 *et seq.*). Although they have taken on human shape and with their cornucopia and other Mediterranean attributes such as a tortoise give the impression of being Mercury and Copia (PL. 176) their pre-Roman, 'barbaric' faces, their squatting posture with their heels tucked under (PL. 182) and, above all, the animals which accompany them, fresh from the scarcely cleared forests of Gaul, show clearly that they do not belong to the Roman divine family, still less to Olympus. In Pl. 190 the hunter-god emerges in ingenuous nudity with his hare from the forest.

From another forest the huge bear comes to pay homage to Artio on her throne (Pl. 178). Sirona, bearing fruit and eggs, has her arms entwined with serpents. In a British bronze of about the same date from Wiltshire, Epona has similar living bracelets, but in our Gallic examples she appears like a Nereid surrounded by marine monsters (Pl. 179) or, later on, like a Roman lady on a smart palfrey; she is not always actually riding but sometimes as in Pl. 180 enthroned, face to the beholder, with her hand laid on the head of the horse or foal and carrying a wreath of foliage, a fit female counterpart, with her severe expression, to the no less impressive hammer-god Sucellos; his ample locks and full beard (Pl. 172) are in the genuine Celtic mode. Esus the woodman is the master of hard pioneering labour (Pl. 173–4). But Cernunnos has remained a man-beast, a denizen of the Gallic forest, old before the Romans' time; horns grow from his head like those of Herne the Hunter, branching out into regular antlers (Pl. 175). At Reims he squats on his throne, a club in one hand, his thick neck encircled with the princely torc, the central figure of an altar-carving, a bull and a stag at his feet, over which a hunter's net falls. The exotic gods Mercury and Apollo merely stand by his side. Traces of the antlers are still visible above his head, distinguishing him from mere men (Pl. 177). We are in the realm of the Matronae, the Great Mothers, that trinity who sit (Pl. 188) all-powerful on earth, taking mankind under their aegis already in his infancy. But human strength is manifest in the horseman, the forefeet of whose mount are trampling down a giant with a hunch back (Pl. 184 & 185). This group often occurs in North and Central Gaul, and has been mistaken for the triumph of Rome (the horseman) over the shapeless barbarian giant. But this group must be seen from the Celtic point of view, not the Roman perspective, by rights. Certainly the rider has some attributes of Jove the Thunderer or Mars in his armour, and his victory over the monster symbolizes the triumph of life over death. But Ferdinand Benoit has lately shown the horseman to be Taranis or Teutates, cardinal Celtic divinities, and the club-footed or legless giant to be the infernal champion of the underworld rising out of the ground. In any case, the group typifies the dualistic duel over the heads of mankind, in which the equestrian god on his leaping horse beats the earth-bound giant. The final proof of the important role played by the horse in the life of the Gauls who had remained an equestrian aristocracy ever since they left Central Europe, is that, placed between the contending anthropomorphic forces, it is itself the instrument of victory. In Britain we see this motif only in the standard regimental tombstones of Roman cavalrymen (Colchester, Gloucester).

When the new faith of the Son of God Made Man spread westwards through the Roman Empire, animals in late Gallo-Roman art still played an important part, with manifold meanings. We should not forget, even though we are dealing with the last manifestation of the classical tradition, that the imagery of the Old and of the New Testaments is essentially that of oriental literature, even though their messages burst all geographical confines for ever. They employ simile and metaphor, the figure known to the Greeks as allegory. Thus the very earliest Christian sarcophagi found on Gallic soil, known by the name of their site as La Gayole, show the Good Shepherd with the sheep on his shoulders, followed by other sheep (Pl. 227, 228). In the shepherd, calling the trusting flock to him (Pl. 239), the faithful saw Jesus just as He had described Himself; but the image also reminds him of the thrice-repeated command to Peter: 'Feed my sheep, feed my lambs." Even the story of the sacrifice of Abraham portrays the Messiah who is to come and ransom mankind by his sacrificial death, in the guise of the ram, which the patriarch after resisting temptation is to offer instead of his beloved son; the ram is represented caught in the branches by its horns, exactly as in the words of scripture (Pl. 240). A later treatment shows the ram on an engraved plaque exactly symmetrical with Isaac (Pl. 253). But in the New Testament the lamb represents the Son of God, *agnus dei*: standing up, in simple outline, which derives from classical forms, again carved on a marble slab (Pl. 252). Again as a carving in relief suggesting movement, the head turned up towards the Throne, on the right hand of whose occupant St John is seen; this is the vision described in the fifth chapter of Revelation, where the lamb possesses the book with seven seals (Pl. 256), a direct foreshadowing of the apocalyptic art of the early Middle Ages. As a more earthy symbol of the burden laid on Eve the lamb appears again in company with our guilty first parents under the branches of the Tree of Knowledge, before they are cast out of Paradise in their guilt (Pl. 233).

A more mysterious oriental legacy of fable, taken over by the new faith, is Christ disguised as the phœnix (Pl. 229), that bird of the desert that rises from the pyre which it has built itself and can be taken as the symbol of resurrection to eternal life. Daniel standing unarmed between two lions goes right back to the epic Sumerian figure of Gilgamesh who overcame the lion and the bull (Pl. 232); but this attitude of prayer between the angel whom the Lord sends to him and the king of the Medes who watched through the night on his account, signifies for the faithful of the young congregations' steadfastness in prayer, that will overcome even the lion which is the peril of death. One of the most frequent images on sarcophagi is therefore the suppliant with outstretched arms (Pl. 228, 230, 231).

Nor are animals wanting from gospel narrative. They stand about the crib at the Nativity, although neither the short report of Matthew nor the more circumstantial account by Luke gives any hint of their presence (Pl. 236, 238). This is derived from apocryphal accounts which influenced pictures of the Nativity and the childhood of Jesus throughout the Middle Ages. The scene did not become fixed in early Christian art; besides the ox and the ass, today traditionally associated with the Christmas crib, we find a magnificant he-goat (Pl. 236). The doves, which the parents of the Lord brought to the Temple at the Presentation as the appropriate gift of the poor as laid down by the Law, the doves as symbols of the pure heart and of good will, are associated with the Chi-Ro monogram of Christ (Pl. 255). We would draw attention again to the fish, whose name in Greek—*ichthys*—forms an acrostic for the Greek words standing for Jesus Christ (the) Son of God (Our) Saviour; this cryptogram lay at the centre of early Christian imagery, and was mentioned, in connection with the allegory of water as the renewer of life, also, together with the loaves miraculously multiplied by Christ, as a foreshadowing of the daily eucharistic miracle (Pl. 243, 244).

Apart from the Latin pun *gallus*, meaning both cock and Gaul, the cock occurs in its simpler gospel context. It stands between Jesus, raising two fingers in adjuration, and Peter, who clutches his beard in alarm and protests against the prophecy of his betrayal (Pl. 245). But it is already perched, crowing, in the tree behind the apostle, who despite his protestations denies his master. But disregarding his human weakness Jesus has entrusted the keys of Heaven to this very apostle (Pl. 246).

In the series of early Christian sarcophagi, the last of all, chronologically, show among the decorative sculptural scenes from the Old and the New Testaments a story at first sight quite foreign to this setting, unmistakably borrowed from the repertoire of pagan antiquity; the hunt of Meleager. The grisly beast that the Greek hero slays is the boar let loose by Artemis on the Etolians because Meleager's father had cheated her of the sacrifice of first-fruits. The story of Artemis and its ramifications had been known in southern Gaul since the first coming of the Greeks; and here the sarcophagus was found. The conquest of the wild beast can be taken by itself simply to typify the victory over death, and what else should the pictures on the outside of a tomb portray? But in Gaul the boar stood for one of the oldest native deities, the image of paganism, conquered by the Christian faith. But further, Oeneus, father of Meleager, had received the primeval vine from Dionysos, so that the hunter can also figure as the heir and transmitter of a symbol that can be interpreted in Christian terms. Such are the means whereby, transferred and purified, the animal world contributed, even in Gaul, to the symbolic illustration of the teaching of the new faith.

THREATENED EXISTENCE

IN CONTRAST to an outmoded historiography which exhausts itself in war-reporting and an endless cataloguing of battles, the history of civilization brings into relief against a background of political strife the positive achievements of humanity. The concept of the heroic has given place to another and happier one: instead of murderous rancour the constructive effect of tradition has become the worthy theme of history. Nothing is farther from our minds than to go against this praiseworthy tendency. Yet, without missing something essential, we cannot avert our eyes from the fact, that of the long periods of time with which we are concerned here, only a short stretch was occupied by the *Pax Romana* in Gaul which assured and ennobled human existence, and that this short respite was bought at a great cost. It was preceded by the immigration of the Celts, so renowned for their skill at arms and war-like nature, and their conflict with the subjection of the previous inhabitants. Are not the ages of classical history full of dark passages chronicling the campaigns of other Celtic hordes in Italy? The conflict of the more southerly Gaulish vanguards with the Greeks who had established themselves all along the Mediterranean coast as traders, and who as a maritime people needed the freedom of the harbours they had sought out and developed for themselves, brought the Romans on to the scene. This let loose a series of martial events the climax of which Caesar himself described as the Gallic War. Rome opposed its own imperialist pressure of expansion to the migratory urge of the Celts, typified in the wanderings of the Helvetii, and this clash of interests led to the intervention of Caesar. This led to much bloodshed, culminating in the subjection of the Gaulish tribes once and for all. All the cruelty was not on the part of the 'barbarians'—now a term of opprobrium with us but for the Romans a simple statement of the fact that foreigners did not speak Latin—Vercingetorix at his ignoble end was a victim of this cruelty which dishonoured the victors.

Even the keenest admirer of things Celtic cannot deny that the spread of Roman civilization brought a more moral way of life to the very shores of the Atlantic, the North Sea, and the Channel. In the place of the blood feud which obliged the head-hunter to kill the enemy of his clan and has left behind grisly memorials in the shape of trophies of skulls, the Roman citizen built his right to existence on a system of written laws. Disregarding all material improvements which do not of themselves necessarily bring any moral advancement to mankind, the concept of written law implies an advancement in the ethical level which was no less a preparation for Christianity than the native Celtic religious temperament.

Caesar and all his successors not only in Gaul but throughout the Empire who followed up the work of conquest with that of pacification—we think of Augustus, Vespasian, Trajan, Hadrian, and the wise Marcus Aurelius, and later of M. Aurelius Probus, Diocletian, the two Constantii, and Constantine—prepared the geographical area in which until the discovery and conquest of new continents western civilization so splendidly unfolded itself, and in which the wandering barbarian tribes were tamed and ennobled.

But for Gaul in particular this meant a period of peace followed by another trouble era. The forts along the Rhine, the relics of the Limes, the transformation of Roman cities into strongholds whose fortified walls were often hastily patched up out of the remains of theatres, structures like the mighty protective Porta Nigra (see PL. 166) all bear witness to the disturbances which interrupted peaceful construction, and to the bitter frontier wars of the Empire. These wars are justified by the fact that the Romans in alliance with the subject Celts were able to make headway against this new attack for so long that finally when the Germans broke in they found a province with its own uniform, stable, durable culture, where they were able by intermarriage with Romanized Celts to become, not destructive barbarians, but settled, constructive builders of a new Frankish civilization; this long defensive war is the fruit of the glorious Gallo-Roman mission without which the West as we know it could not have come into being.

But the temporal struggle for power that resulted in the Roman Empire is overshadowed by a much more extensive spiritual conflict. We do not reckon the passage of the years from the days of Julius Caesar who made way for the Empire and established its future greatness. Although he regarded himself as a god and shook the foundations of the known world, he was, viewed on a higher plane, only the agency by which the space was cleared for Him who is God Himself and redeemed the world. Half a century after the Ides of March, that day of destiny on which Caesar succumbed to the conspiracy of his enemies and of some of those who thought themselves his friends, the Prince of Peace appeared in an out-of-the-way corner of the Empire and erected without the slightest historical splendour, only through the proclaiming of his mission of salvation, through His death freely suffered on the cross, and His resurrection which the Roman armed power could not prevent, His kingdom which is not of this world. And yet—'Render unto Caesar the things that are Caesar's'—the gospel of Jesus Christ was spread first through the empire of Rome. In Gaul too His messengers trod the roads that the legions had built and maintained, abode in the cities that the Romans had sited and laid out and preached his doctrine within the framework of Roman culture. The periods during which the Christians were persecuted connects Gaul with the heroic infancy of Christianity, for the faith was not totally accepted there, on the contrary that soil which for centuries had been watered with the blood of dying soldiers now was sanctified with that of the martyrs spilt in violent death.

The pictures which follow bear abundant witness of these manifold dangers, of these wars in which the aggressors became the attacked, and at the end of which only the power of the spirit remained alive. Even on the threshold of history we see the pre-Celtic inhabitants of Gaul as armed men, sculptured in the menhir statues. The hilltop settlements prove by their barely accessible sites, chosen by the Celts or taken over by them from earlier inhabitants such as the Ligurians in the South, how much mankind felt threatened in its existence, enough to supplement the defnciencies of natural defences by building mighty walls (Pl. 23) of mixed timber, earth, and stone, the typical 'Gallic walls' of the interior such as Caesar described in his account of the siege of Avaricum (Commentaries, Book 7, Cap. 23). These were imitated from the unmixed masonry that protected the Greek coastal settlements and trading ports. Finds of the La Tène period include weapons besides the coins, pottery, metal tools, and jewellery. Even in the urns of Ensérune iron swords were buried with the warriors.

It is then no matter for wonder that in the sculpture of the Celts and of the Mediterranean tribes with whom they mingled the figure of the warrior should appear so often. Side by side with the gods and demons, princes and princesses, with the uncovered heads that are memorials of the dead we show helmeted heads from the lower Rhône. The historically important explanation of the military equipment of the tribes who at the time of their penetration of the area gave the Greeks so much trouble and whom the Romans were to combat later on, is matched by the artistic interest, for these works exhibit with exaggerated firmness that severity of form which we have tried to analyse when commenting on the sculptured heads of Roquepertuse and Entremont. The two busts of warriors from St-Anastasie near Gardon north-west of Nîmes (Pl. 41 & 42) with their huge, almost roof-like leather helmets, with sweeping curves and decorated rims, and under them long, narrow-cheeked faces, strongly ridged brows, mouths firmly shut in straight lines and heavily modelled chins, bear a stony expression of mortal resolve. The expression on these faces explain phrases like Caesar's 'Suddenly war broke out in Gaul' and what they must have meant for the Romans, and why Caesar in spite of himself resorted to such reprisals as the lopping off of hands reported by Hirtius. What heroic resolve is expressed in the flung-back head resting on the massive neck in the bust from Entremont (Pl. 43), stiffly framed in the close-fitting helmet with ear-and-neck guards. Near Nîmes, too, at Grezan, was found a warrior in helmet and armour (Pl. 44). The headdress which comes down to the shoulders gives further protection to the ears. The neck, thick as ever, bears a torc, and the belted loins are narrow. Geometrical patterns adorn the square breastplate. There is no mail-shirt: instead, an unpleated buff coat hangs without a fold in the stiff leather from shoulders to mid-thigh, on a warrior's torso from Entremont, severely damaged but recognizably in a crouching attitude, perhaps riding (Pl. 46). It must be that of a warrior because of the pectoral, the narrow belt, and the sword hanging along the right thigh. A slightly receding plane below the breastplate shows how the upper part was drawn over the lower. Another torso, likewise from Entremont, wears a very well-preserved breastplate. Between the downward-rolled spirals of a geometrical design appears a severed head (Pl. 143, 169) like the Medusa's head of a classical gorgonion. With this typical Celto-Ligurian element the circle of our observations is complete; this symbol sums up the defensive attitude of the Celts to external dangers. The fighting man protects himself with the image of victory, the head-trophy, and at the same time seeks to terrify his enemy by a picture of the decapitation that awaits him.

For all that the Celtic tribes of Gaul, so singularly lacking in a sense of political unity that even in their hour of greatest peril they were unwilling to subject themselves to the overall command of Vercingetorix, the one chief who was resolved to resist *à outrance* and who might have imposed the solidarity that would have saved them all, were forced to capitulate to the superior Roman forces—not numerically superior indeed but centrally directed by Caesar who combined a strategic technique of genius with diplomatic cunning. At the end of the Gallic War, Caesar reported: 'Defessam tot adversis proeliis Galliam . . . facile in pace continuit.' From the day in 102 B.C. when the republican general Marius repulsed the Cimbri and Teutones in the plain of the little River Arc near the village of Pourrières, the migration of the barbarians was halted for centuries to come and the fate of Gaul was sealed. Henceforth the Gallic warrior figures in Roman sculpture as a manacled captive, led side by side with fur-clad German prisoners on triumphal arches and city gates. PL. 75, 103 are typical memorials of the occupying power, where swords of Celtic forging hang as trophies of the victor. There was nothing the Romans loved better than to perpetuate their successes in tangible form.

The triple arch of Orange, built in the time of Augustus but reinscribed under Tiberius, bears witness in that very Rhône valley where the Romans were at first twice defeated by the barbarians, in PL. 101 & 102, to their ultimate victory. It bears the image of the defeated chieftains and names them: Udillo, Dacurdo, Avot, Mario; but in a more general way it depicts the Roman superiority by land (PL. 101) and by sea (PL. 102). Massilia, too, which had backed Pompey instead of Caesar in the Civil War, had to submit to the neighbouring power on which it had once called for help. In both cases the sculptured reliefs present a true picture of the armament: shields with painted devices, swords in their sheaths, helmets, bundles of spears, garments, pieces of armour, the whole topped by a single severed head, quite in the Celtic tradition, to denote victory by land, while the beaks of captured Massiliot galleys, the corresponding symbol of naval victory, give a realistic picture of marine architecture. But at the same time these reliefs are splendid examples of the decoration of flat planes where the Roman speciality of low relief is seen at its best. These objects, apparently distributed haphazard, over and under and side by side with each other, are really very artistically arranged to bring out a pattern confidently constructed from the contrast of complementary horizontal, perpendicular, and diagonal surfaces, boldly opposed arching curves, that transcends the mere representational and reaches a peak of abstract composition that is at once modern and primeval but was not to be attained again until the advent of cubism two thousand years later. This is the consummation of Roman art on Gallic soil. Its aesthetic triumph is more permanent than the military victory of which it was the pictorial symbol.

At Avignon two statues have been preserved (PL. 186 & 187) in which the Celtic warrior appears again, in the Gallo-Roman era. Beyond the arrogance of victory and the humiliation of defeat, as if withdrawn above the battle, at once confidently erect and relaxed as he leans on his tall shield, he wears a fringed cloak that falls almost to the ground over the shield (compare this typical Celtic garment with those in Pl. 101, top right, and Pl. 103, the figure on the left) and a mail-shirt whose invention has been ascribed to this nation of ironworkers, a metal torc round his neck—the very literal model of a statue, which means 'standing image.' One of them comes from Vacheres high up in the Alps where according to the latest discoveries there must have been an important centre of Celto-Ligurian resistance. The other—which has no head—comes from Mondragon in the Rhône valley, down which wave after wave of barbarians surged against the dam of the Roman legions. The details of this pitiless clash we can see in a dramatic and dynamic relief at Trier near the frontier of the Rhine (Pl. 164).

The statue of Mars, god of war, leaning against a pillar in Lutetia as if wounded, brings home to one what this long century of military effort must have meant to the Romans themselves, fighting now not for loot or military renown, but to preserve the very existence of their threatened empire for themselves and the peoples allied to them, to preserve the higher values, the enduring benefits of the *Pax Romana*. 'Nations of the earth, acknowledge your good fortune, being subjects of the Roman Empire,' says the younger Pliny in his panegyric of the Emperor Trajan. In Pl. 169 the son of Jupiter, and father of the city, founder Romulus appears in the regulation armour of the Roman legionary, but his body is not in the stiff regimental position of attention, but relaxed at the hips in an almost affected and completely unmilitary attitude characteristic of Roman civilian statues. Elegance, too, is expressed in the negligent diagonal disposition of the arms—the lowered right arm complementary to the left which is clasping the spear shaft high up. The head, slightly bent and framed in locks of hair beneath the helmet with its uncanny death mask—compare the genuine Roman face-visor in Pl. 160—expresses with its dreamy distance-seeking gaze and its weakly-formed, disillusioned mouth a strange melancholy, mourning over the inexorable fate that overshadows even the immortal god in his mortal human form. For the Roman who can enjoy the pleasures of life but also knows spiritual happiness, war means only hard necessity in which he takes no joy, and death is for him the inevitable tragedy of all human existence.

'Fight to remain what philosophy has made you. Honour the gods, help yourself. Life is short.' This short rule, this wisdom wrung from the knowledge of how transitory all earthly things can be, has been cast by a Roman emperor into Greek phrases: they are to be found in the sixth book of the Meditations of Marcus Aurelius, the prologue to the portrait of his adoptive father and predecessor which the stoic in the purple set up as an example to himself. Whether the golden bust (Pl. 143) found at Aventicum portrays Antoninus or Aurelius, it is worth while to spend a few moments in contemplation of this human image. Cannot one read in its noble features what Marcus demands of himself? . . . 'He wills no other thing but to keep the right path according to the law, and to follow God who marks out that path.'

If proof were needed of the deep seriousness with which thinking men in antiquity sought to answer the eternal questions, which destiny put to them, it would suffice to point out that philosophy to this day is indebted to the thought of ancient times, that the human spirit is even now repeatedly catching the spark from Aristotle and Plato. It was Rome, here as in other spheres of knowledge, that managed the diffusion of the Greek heritage throughout the earth. Its own powers of original creation were in the political, the social, the economic spheres, but it was Rome that created and preserved order, which alone assured life, throughout a geographical space immeasurable by the standards of those times. That it was able significantly to fulfil this task, is due in considerable measure to its adoption of Greek ways of thought. Those who have to grapple with existence must come to terms with its problems. Valid material solutions are always the result of asking oneself the right intellectual questions.

If thoughtfully we peruse the last section of these illustrations, if we let the familiar biblical scenes make their effect in this late classical form, if we try to capture the significance of attitude and facial expression, and see how nobly they combine to bring the eternal verities before us, how on the marble tomb of the dead they point beyond the short life of this earth, we are naturally led to consider the spirit that gives them the form they have preserved to this day but which in the last event is transitory also. What was hinted at in the primitive masks, attempted in the Celtic heads, indicated in the Roman busts, here finds its fulfilment. In Pl. 248 and 249 the apostles look each other in the eye, turned to each other in dumb dialogue. For whom are their unspoken words meant? In Pl. 247 we ourselves look into the astonished eyes of one of them. If we could only catch the words that have given his stone countenance the calm of certainty, the dignity of confidence. We are not of the stature to transcribe them. Rather let us hear the words written on the stone of Autun, that dictate a fitting conclusion to this essay. It is the beginning of the inscription of Pectorios, done late in the second century, but the earliest Christian testimony in Gaul, carved by the founder to accompany his dear father Archandios, his mother, and his brothers into eternal life. 'Heavenly kindred of the divine Fish, fortify your hearts, for you have found in the midst of things mortal the immortal source of the divine waters.'

The Threshold of History

1 Dolmen at Nouaillaguet (Creuse). Megalithic centre of barrow, consisting of seven uprights and flat lintel. Second or third millenium B.C. Height from ground level 2 m., length 5 m., width 3½ m. Interior depth 1 m. Situated about three miles north-west of the village.

2 Sacrificial Stone at Perseix (Creuse). Altar-shaped megalith with two round scooped-out grooves of unequal breadth and a narrow ridge between them. Second or third millennium B.C. Popularly called 'Fauteuil du Diable' (The Devil's Armchair) which is perhaps a corruption of 'Autel du Diable' (The Devil's Altar) suggested by the shape of the monument. Such names denote Christian hostility towards pagan remains such as the megalithic gateway and sacrificial stone near Diekirch in Luxemburg, similarly named. Height 1 m. 80. Length and breadth both between 2 and 2½ m. Situated north of the village.

3 Stone of the Nine Steps near Martineiche (Creuse). The highest of several such blocks, all more or less hewn with tools, forming a crown round the summit of a hill that falls sharply away on all sides (some 1,800 feet high) to the south of the village. The block has been levelled off smoothly at the top but for two concentric circular grooves of unequal width joined by a short, round, accurately bored tunnel through the narrow ridge between them. Numerous other blocks lying near by have been worked to give them a characteristic symmetrical 'monumental' form. Maximum height of block at rear 4 m., height of staircase 1½ m.

4 Menhir Statue of Mas Capellier (Aveyron). Stylized human figure of the declining megalithic period. Either a sling or some ornament of the chest between chin and belt. Some of these menhir statues found in the *massif central* are as much as 2 m. high; there are a dozen of them in the museum at Rodez (Aveyron). Native stone, 73 cm. × 40 cm. × 17 cm. Musée des Antiquités Nationales, St Germain-en-Laye (Seine-et-Oise). Hereinafter M.A.N.

5 Menhir Statue at Puech-Real (Tarn). Human figure like that in 4. The object hanging from the right shoulder towards the belt is interpreted either as a weapon (sword or dagger) or as fire-kindling tool (by A. Varagnac). Native stone. Height 85 cm., width 38 cm., depth 17 cm. Relief nowhere deeper than 2 cm.

The Art of the Celts and Their Predecessors

6 The Boar-God of Euffigneix (Haute-Marne). Although this is probably only of the Gallo-Roman period, it has been dated earlier, and is a continuation of the menhir-statue tradition by virtue of its stone-bound lines (compare 4 and 5 above) but at the same time the work is reminiscent of wood-carving and in overall composition and in detail is purely 'Celtic': mixture of the human form with animal figures, incorporated in the god. Stylized face still recognizable despite mutilation; shape of eyes, height of ears, massive neck, hair-style (so far as this is preserved), necklace or *torques*. Alongside the limbless trunk, instead of arms huge eyes, exactly as long as the boar and disposed on the same axis as the latter. Native stone, height 26 cm., breadth 8 cm., depth 6 cm. M.A.N.

7 Detail of 6 above, horizontally disposed for comparison with 8.

8 Boar from Neuvy-en-Sullias (Loiret). Belongs to a group of large, medium, and small bronze statuary found here. At the time of the Roman occupation, these sacred objects were hidden on the left bank of the Loire opposite their central sanctuary which lay on the right bank near the modern St Benoit-sur-Loire (Floriacum, Fleury), perhaps in face of a threatened migration. The boar is one of the sacred animals of the Celts, a creature of the Other World. The high ridge of bristles, the lines of the head, the braced feet, the virile outline of the body, are all typical of Celtic stylization. Bronze. Height 68 cm., length 1 m. 26, width 33 cm. Musée Historique Orléanais, Orleans (Loiret).

9 MASK OF A CELTIC GOD, FROM THE PYRENEES. Only the nose and the mouth have been beaten out of the smooth, curved metal surface. The eyes have been sawn out, to form a foreheadless face. Hair is indicated by embossed spirals, beard by S-curves, the rims of the eyes (lashes?) by scratched lines. Most striking feature is the bulging hair, drawn on either side. The empty eye-sockets, according to R. Lantier, were originally filled in with glass, enamel, or semi-precious stones. Third century B.C. Bronze. Height 17.2 cm., width 11½ cm., depth 7½ cm. Tarbes Museum (Hautes-Pyrénées).

10 SECTOR OF EXCAVATIONS AT ENSÉRUNE (Hérault). This Gallic fortified town or *oppidum*, situated on a hill falling steeply towards the Mediterranean, between Béziers and Narbonne, gives the clearest picture of a hilltop site continuously occupied from neolithic times to the Roman invasion, fortified several times over and used by several successive waves of population. Prehistoric, Celtic (principally the latter, as shown here) and Roman remains bear witness to the superposition of successive cultures. A museum contains finds from numerous urn-burials. In the third century B.C. the *oppidum* attained its greatest extent of some 750 m. by 300 m. and a population of about eight thousand.

11 THE GOD FROM BOURAY (Seine-et-Oise). This squatting figure with legs tucked under it, a god in human form but with the feet of a stag (compare with the stag-god Cernunnos (PL. 175 & 177), wears a neck-ring of Celtic design with clubbed ends like the boar-god of Euffigneix. The arms are missing. The left eye, which alone has survived, is a typical Celtic inlay. Varied datings have been given: third century according to the Schaffhausen catalogue, second or first century B.C. according to Lantier-Hubert. Bronze. Both head and body are made of separate front and back parts, the joints being visible at the rising of the neck and at the sides. Height 45 cm., width 25 cm. depth 10 cm. M.A.N.

12 DETAIL OF HEAD FROM 11.

13 FRIEZE OF FOUR HORSES' HEADS, FROM ROQUEPERTUSE (Bouches-du-Rhône). Relief produced by deep carving round the outlines, from the shrine discovered on this site. It was probably a fragment of a gateway-statue (compare 26, 28 and 29). Beside the three profiles to the left, the fourth head, on the right, is shown full-face, both nostrils being visible. F. Benoit interprets this frieze as possibly a representation of the Ride of the Dead. Third to second century B.C. Reddish stone from Coudoux (north of Roquepertuse) with traces of colouring. Height 34 cm., breadth 63 cm., depth 33 cm. Musée Borely, Marseilles.

14 DOUBLE-HEADED GOD FROM ROQUEPERTUSE. Part of the gateway to the shrine. Between and above the two bald skulls remains of a gigantic bird's beak, which seems to be holding the sculpture. (Compare figure of a bird in 28.) At the back of the carving a wedge was preserved with which the block was fastened to larger monument. Third century B.C. Stone from Coudoux. Height of heads, 21 cm., width 13 cm., distance from nose to nose, 34 cm. Fragment of beak 13 cm. high. Musée Borely, Marseilles.

15 LEFT HEAD FROM 14.

16 HEAD IN RELIEF, FROM MONTSALLEIR (Basses-Alpes). Bust representing a corpse. Undeciphered inscription in Greek letters on plinth. The head was originally flanked by two scenes, of which only the one on the left has survived. It shows a female figure in a long robe, escorted by two men in short clothes, one with a sword at his belt. Perhaps a picture of the journey to the Other World, otherwise presented as the Death Ride or a voyage in the Ship of the Dead. Tool-marks on the under-surface of the block indicate that is was an architrave, resting on columns. Unmistakably Celtic to judge by the stylization of the face and certain hall-marks such as the position of the ears, but date uncertain. Native stone. Height 11 cm. (15 including plinth), width at height of eyes, 7½ cm., relief 2 cm. deep. Probable length of block 60 cm. Musée Borely, Marseilles.

17 Rock Fortress of Rocsaliere (Vaucluse). West wall of the 'Druids Temple,' one of the outer fortified rock-peaks of the extensive *oppidum* which covers a high plateau south of Apt (Apt Julia). At base, clear traces of natural bulwark reinforced by man-made masonry; higher up, post-holes, of which there are many round the peak. On the left, the deep valley of the River Calavon, Vaucluse plateau in background.

18 Rear Entrance to Rock Fortress, accessible by stone-built stairway about 3 m. high. The entrance itself is blocked by three courses of stonework so that a man would be under cover in the passage-way hewn out behind it. Putlog holes at left over timber gateway. Remains of fortifications to left stairway.

19 Pre-Roman Road on the High Plateau of Claparedes (Vaucluse). The kerb has been preserved on the left of the road-bed which is stone-paved and just under two metres wide. Site between Saignon and Sivergues.

20 Profile of Road in 19. The horizontal paving stones are about 1 metre above ground-level, held in place and protected by a kerb of vertical flags of uniform size, giving the effect of a causeway running across the plateau, dry and capable of bearing traffic in all seasons.

21 Wall Ornament in the Celtic Tradition above the Road, from Auribeau Saignon (Vaucluse). The excellent state of preservation makes it seem probable that this stone 'signpost' which serves to make a crossroad visible from a long way off has been repaired or improved in later times. Some of the upright flags still crown the top of the wall. Identical wall-ornaments are found both sides of the Calavon: on the ruins of a house at Glanum, north of Dijon, at many places in the neighbourhood of Cahors on the Lot, and on heights overlooking the Mediterranean west of Toulon: all places where the remains of round houses such as 22 have been found.

22 Round House of the Pre-Celtic Tradition in Dry-stone Walling on the plateau of Claparedes (Vaucluse), between Saignon and Sivergues. Built without mortar or windows, lit and accessible only by the three-foot-high doorway with its doorpost of rectangular hewn stone in one piece. Height $3\frac{1}{2}$ m., outer diameter at base 4 m., walls from 60 cm. to 1 m. thick. But some individual buildings were up to 5 m. high and 6 m., across with walls more than a metre thick. Reminiscent of the beehive cells of early Irish monasteries (Skellig, etc.). Objects found under the floors of such houses often go back to late Neolithic times and range through Bronze and Iron Ages to the Roman occupation. Often the houses were occupied again as refuges during such times of crisis as the Migration of Peoples, Saracen raids, Wars of Religion, etc. Similar round houses are also common on the southern slopes of the Cevennes; called variously bories, claparedes, capitelles, cabanons pointus.

23 Outer Wall of the Oppidum of Entremont (Bouches-du-Rhône). On the right a section of the wall, on the left one of the projecting, slightly rounded fortified towers of the great bastion on the north side of this Celto-Ligurian town. The hole above the bushes is not an opening, but the place where one of the stones fell out of the wall. Third century B.C. Height 4 m.

24 Upper Town of Entremont. View of a sector of the excavations to date on the site which was not only a town but a religious sanctuary of the Salii or Saluvii, lying to the north of and above Aix-en-Provence. On the left, entrance to a house; on the right storage pit. On the outside corners of the houses stones and flags were left protruding to protect the structure from jostling wagons. The building technique is the same dry-walling with flagstones as in the pre-Celtic round houses. Compare 22. Destroyed by the Romans in 123 B.C. Excavations in progress.

25 Head-stone from Entremont. Upper part of an originally vertical pillar (as in photograph)

decorated with twelve heads, which was later used as a threshold to the 'Hall of the Heads' at the Celto-Ligurian shrine of Entremont. Third century B.C. at latest. Limestone. Height (now length) of the whole stone 1 m. 60 cm. Breadth 34 cm. in this section. Depth 43 cm. at base, 41 cm. in upper part. Heads measure 25, 24, 24, 23 cm., in height, and 17, 16, 16, 15 cm., in width (in descending order). The other heads, not illustrated here, were arranged in twos and threes and varied in height from 21 to 15 cm., and in width from 13 to 10 cm.

26 Skull Stone from Entremont. Fragments of a stone doorpost with skull-niches (also on reverse side), and a deeply imbedded relief of a head, which was perhaps provisional to be replaced by a real skull inserted as a trophy. Third century B.C. Limestone. Height 40 cm. Length of fragment 75 cm., breadth 35 to 37 cm. Niches measure 25 to 19 cm. high (at rear) 18 to 24 cm. broad, relief 1½ cm. deep. Lying in the 'Hall of Heads' in the shrine.

27 Stone with Serpent Relief from Entremont. Also used as threshold to 'Hall of Heads.' Limestone post, 42 cm. high, 1 m. 23 long, 48 cm. broad. Snake 66 cm. long.

28 Original Door-frame, from Roquepertuse (Bouches-du-Rhône). Three pillars with skull-niches one above the other for heads of enemies or skulls of native heroes used as relics. Above the door-frame a bird ready to fly, symbol of the journey to the Other World. Pillars show traces of decorative paintings of fish and foliage. Third century B.C. Reddish stone from Coudoux. Approximate measurement as reconstructed: height, 2½ m., breadth 2½ m. Pillars originally measured 40 cm. square. Musée Borely, Marseilles.

29 Frieze with Heads and Horses, from Nages (Gard). Stone beams like door-lintel. Under the cornice, probable representation of dead man—the eyes are slit-like, almost closed—and the horses of the ride of the dead. Second century B.C. Limestone. Overall measurement 50 cm. high, 1 m. 42 long. Frieze alone: 26 cm. high, 1 m. 28 long, relief 1½ to 2 cm. deep. Head on left 22 cm. high, 18 cm. wide. Head on right, 22 cm. high, 17 cm. wide. Horse on left 23 cm. high, 30 cm. long. Horse on right 22 cm. high, 32 cm. long. Archaeological Museum, Nîmes (Gard).

30 Stone Block with Two Heads in Relief, from Entremont. Right-hand surface of a block of stone, probably fragment of a pillar, bearing a mounted figure in relief on the front, riding towards the right and carrying a lance, and on the left surface a single head, with the back left blank. Third or second century B.C. Limestone, 40 cm. high, 40 cm. long, breadth as shown 38 cm. Musée Granet, Aix-en-Provence (Bouches-du-Rhône).

31 The Monster of Noves (Bouches-du-Rhône). The anthropophagous beast sits on its hind legs which are stretched forwards, two bearded human heads balanced on them, the forepaws resting on these heads. Between its chin and right forepaw a human arm with bracelet. Above the left forepaw a fragment of a human foot (evidently a leg, worn away now, led from here to the mouth of the monster) The monster, well known under the name of 'Tarasque de Noves' is covered along the back from head to loins with scales. Five ribs can be seen on one side. The tail lies along the right hind foot. Pre-Roman. Native stone. Height, 1 m. 12, breadth 55 m., depth 71 cm. Head of monster 20 cm. high, 30 cm. broad, 44 cm. deep. Heads under the paws 30 cm. high. Lapidarium of Musée Calvet, Avignon, Vaucluse.

32 Head with Hand Laid on it, from Entremont. The face was no doubt mutilated by the Romans after the destruction of the shrine of the Salii. Limestone. Height including hand 29 cm., breadth 17 cm., depth to point where wrist was broken off 21 cm. Musée Granet, Aix-en-Provence.

33 Left Head from 31.

34 Head (of a Child) with Hand Laid Sideways, from Entremont. A lock of hair falls down over the back of the hand coming between thumb and index finger. The head is split vertically and the right half is incomplete. Limestone 25 cm. high, 15 cm. broad without the missing portion, depth to point where wrist breaks off 25 cm. Musée Granet, Aix-en-Provence.

35 Seated Human Figure with Legs Tucked Under, from Roquepertuse (Bouches-du-Rhône.) God, priest, prince or deified hero. Wearing torc and arm-ring. Head, right arm and left hand broken off. The robe covering the torso from breast to loins has been hacked away so that the body looks disproportionately slim. Third century B.C. Stone from Coudoux. One metre high, 54 cm. broad at shoulders, depth at legs 67 cm. Plinth shows traces of acrotery (angular decoration) Musée Borely, Marseilles.

36 Human Figure, from Roquepertuse, as 35. Wearing robe decorated above with lozenge pattern, lower down with finely pointed lines, a belt and a cloak like a chasuble with step-like folds on the chest, hanging down to the belt behind.

37 Head of Prince, from Entremont. Hair evenly drawn back to nape of neck, and over it, reaching from ear to ear, a diadem; fine modelling of occiput. Stone diadem imitates woven metal original. Head broken off a bust or statue, nose mutilated. Limestone, 28 cm. high, 19 cm. broad, 22 cm. deep. Musée Granet, Aix-en-Provence.

38 Human Head with Curly Hair, from Entremont. Broken off, no headgear. Nose and right cheek mutilated. Limestone. Height 28 cm., breadth 18 cm., depth 22 cm. Musée Granet, Aix-en-Provence.

39 Female Head, from Entremont. Hair completely covered by a cloth which fell down to the shoulders, perhaps even further. Ear rings visible beneath it on both sides. Nose and chin slightly damaged. Traces on right side of neck of repeated attempts to sever head, Second century B.C. at latest, as also 37 and 38. Limestone, 29 cm. high, 18 cm. broad, 24½ cm. deep. In private possession.

40 Stone with Four Heads, from Entremont. Two men's heads with hair combed back, above them two hooded women's heads as in 39. Probably memorial to the dead. Third century B.C. Limestone, 50 cm. high, 32½ cm. broad, but the stone has been broken off on the left. 17 cm. deep. Musée Granet, Aix-en-Provence.

41 Bust of Warrior, from Ste-Anastasie (Gard). Stonework representing huge leather helmet with possibly metal decorations, coming right down to the shoulders. Cloak indicated by transverse strokes. The plinth-like breast-piece shows three faintly scratched horses galloping to the left—the Ride of the Dead. Third century B.C. Native stone. Height 54 cm. Breadth (lower part of helmet) 39 cm. Depth of helmet 30 cm. Measurements of earless face: height 21 cm.; breadth 13 cm. Archaeological Museum at Nîmes.

42 Second Bust of Warrior. Similar to 41 above from same place, but not rear view of the same as has been falsely reported. Features mutilated. Third century B.C. Height 52 cm.; breadth 32 cm.; depth 40 cm. Archaeological Museum at Nîmes.

43 Warrior's Head, from Entremont. Closely fitting helmet (leather?) held round forehead and occiput with circular brim, with flaps either side to protect ears, and one at rear covering nape of neck. Face mutilated, especially nose. Broken off at neck. Second century B.C. at latest. Limestone. Height 32 cm.; breadth 18½ cm.; depth from chin to occiput 24 cm. Musée Granet, Aix-en-Provence.

44 Bust of Warrior, from Grezan (Gard). Probably part of statue. Helmet similar to 41 and 42. In contrast to these and to 46, this warrior is wearing armour that derives from classical prototypes. Gorgoneion (gorget) with geometrical patterns. Face mutilated. Ears, or perhaps leather earflaps visible below helmet. Noticeably thick neck wears torc with flattened terminals to protect the Adam's apple. Native stone. Height 72 cm., breadth 43 cm., depth 30 cm. at chest. Head 19 cm. high, 16 cm.

broad, 31 cm. deep, with helmet. Archaeological Museum, Nîmes.

45 Gorget, from Bust of Warrior, at Entremont. In place of the classical gorgoneion a severed head in ornamental geometrical style imitating metal. Limestone. Height 8½ cm.; breadth 18½ cm.; relief ½ cm. deep. Musée Granet, Aix-en-Provence.

46 Seated (Riding?) Warrior, from Entremont. Wears a close-fitting jerkin of pigskin, covering shoulders and upper arm, and coming down to the upper thigh. Gorget damaged. Broadsword hanging from belt at right side (just visible, left of picture). Torso is in four pieces; head, arms, and lower part of legs broken off. Not later than second century B.C. Limestone. Height 80 cm.; breadth at shoulders 55 cm.; at thighs 62 cm. Depth at chest 30 cm., at left thigh 65 cm. Musée Granet, Aix-en-Provence.

47 Dancing Girl, from Neuvy-en-Sullias (Loiret). Naked as ritual demanded. Right arm partly stretched out, left arm bent back with hand at nape of neck. Hair covered by shawl that falls down behind, to shoulders. Right leg slightly twisted to one side and raised, point of toe touching ground. Celtic of Gallo-Roman period. Cast bronze, 14 cm. high, 8 cm. wide at arms. Musée Historique d'Orléanais, Orleans.

48 Striding or Dancing Man, from Neuvy-en-Sullias. Nude. Left leg forward, right foot on tiptoe, arms slightly raised forward and outwards, probably carrying some object now missing. Features, hair and beard stylized in Celtic manner. Stamped on inner side of right thigh SOVTO or SCUTO. Cast bronze of Gallo-Roman period, 20 cm. high, 10 cm. broad at arms. Musée Orléanais.

49 Jongleur, from Neuvy-en-Sullias. Nude. The movement of the arms and backward-tilted head with cloth on forehead denote profession. As with other Celtic masculine figures of this period the nipples are prominently modelled (cf. 50 and 56). Right knee slightly bent, weight on the left foot, as in 47, 48, 50 and 51. Height 12 cm., breadth at arms 6½ cm. Musée Orléanais.

50 Man Playing Instrument, from Neuvy-en-Sullias. Fully clothed with low slung belt over jerkin. Tightly fitting breeches (bracae). Pattern of material visible also on legs. The arms which are stretched forward, the right one raised, held an instrument which has disappeared, either cymbals or a harp. Right knee raised, right foot missing. Typical Celtic hair style. Cast bronze, 10.3 cm. high, breadth at arms 5 cm. Musée Orléanais.

51 Dancing or Running Woman, from Saint-Laurent-des-Bois (Loir-et-Cher). Nude. Dorsal aspect. Left arm raised with hand slightly bent, right arm stretched forward, hand lost. Long hair falling down the back. Right leg drawn back, foot on tiptoes, Left leg forward, foot on the ground. Assigned on grounds of style and theme to the group of bronze statuettes found at Neuvy-en-Sullias (47–50) although found some distance north-west of there in 1865. 9 cm. high, breadth across arms 3¾cm. Musée Orléanais.

52 Bull's Head, from Near Troyes (Aube). Tips of horns bated with knobs for safety, either at work or for some kind of sport (mock bullfight?). Gallo-Roman period, first century A.D. External breadth between tips of horns 7 cm. Internal breadth 5 cm. Height 7½ cm. Depth 8½ cm. Musée des Beaux-Arts, Troyes.

53 Horse, from Near Chalons-sur-Marne. Belongs to the finds centring on Catalaunum. Off forefoot raised, near hind slightly raised, off-hind and near-forefoot missing on ground. Trotting on left diagonal. Gallo-Roman. Bronze, 17 cm. high, 21 cm. long, 5 cm. broad. Municipal Museum, Chalons. (Compare little bronze horse from Aventicum, 194.)

54 Stag, from Neuvy-en-Sullias (Loiret). All legs rigid, each pair of feet together. Antlers in velvet. Gallo-Roman. Bronze, 34 cm. high, 25 cm. long, 8 cm. broad. Musée Orléanais.

55 Male Mask, from Garancières-en-Beauce (Eur-et-Loire). Head without beard but still fully stylized in Celtic fashion (hair style, high-set ears, arch of brows, nose, mouth, chin). Eyes sawn out of metal, probably once filled in with enamel or semi-precious stones. Striking thick neck. Rather flat mask, open at rear. Eye-sockets are only stopped up for purposes of this photograph. Brass, 9.8 cm. high, breadth at ears 6½ cm.

56 Sitting God, from Mandeur (Doubs). According to a monograph now in preparation by N. Duerr, this work which comes from Epamandodurum, this is a joint representation of Mars and Mercury. The bronze statuette was once gilt and the helmet had a crest, either a boar or a raven. Left hand resting on a shield, which has gone, the right holding a staff which has also gone. Feet damaged by fire. Features typical of Celtic mask. Details such as measurements and exact dating based on clothing to be given in Duerr's work. Height 18½ cm. Historical Museum of Basle.

The Greeks on the Mediterranean Shore

57 Archaic Stele of Artemis, from Massilia (Bouches-du-Rhône). One of forty-one found in the ruins of the temple of Artemis north of the Greek harbour of Marseilles. Of Ionian type, the shape called Naiskos. The goddess of Ephesus who was also tutelary diety of Massilia, seated in a severely hieratic attitude in a cottage-shaped niche, is closely swathed in a robe and has her head hooded in some sort of veil (compare the female head from Entremont, 39) Sixth century B.C. Local limestone. 50 cm. high, 27 cm. broad, 23 cm. deep. Figure of goddess 27½ cm. high. Musée Borely, Marseilles.

58 Hellenistic Stele of Artemis, from Massilia. Besides the numerous archaic steles, one Hellenistic votive tablet found so far shows the goddess erect and unveiled with her gown girt up, the arms raised sideways in a gesture of blessing, the hands resting on the capitals of the two pillars that support the roof of the shrine but in the classical attitude of prayer. The change in the Greek religious conception and artistic sensibility after three centuries of evolution is shown by contrast with 57 and 58. Third or second century B.C. Limestone, 44 cm. high, 30 cm. broad, 17 cm. deep. Figure of goddess 30½ cm. high. Musée Borely, Marseilles.

59–63 Excavations at Saint-Blaise (Bouches-du-Rhône). In the light of research lasting a decade and undertaken by the director of excavations, Henri Rolland (they are still going on), we can see that the site is the Greek town of Mastramele, connected with Marseilles and founded close to a neolithic settlement. Dated by pottery at seventh or perhaps even eighth century B.C., it was a Greek trading post. 60 is a view across the streets and houses of the Tiorlis (state of excavations as at Spring 1957) but overlaid with later buildings. In the fourth century B.C., while the Celts were filtering into the area between the lower Rhône and the Alps, the city was fortified against attack by labourers imported from Sicily with a vast encircling wall and converted into a regular acropolis. Part of this wall shown on right of 59 at base, then above it remains of the later settlement of Ugium, of early Christian date, with (upper left) a dry-stone hut in the style, but built without the archaic craftsmanship, of the pre-Celtic beehive 'cells' (22). Fortified wall in 62 near main gate of Greek town shows Sicilian technique of squared masonry with above and behind it ruins of later settlement. On left, above, outline of blocks rounded by weathering, the same blocks seen from the front in 63. These are the crenellations, monumental and crowning the wall at intervals. In 61 on left is a part of the Greek wall and on right the rounded apse of the early Christian church of St Peter of Ugium (fourth or fifth century). The still unfinished excavations at St Blaise between the salt lakes of Citis and Lavalduc are among the most important sites of archaeological research on Gallic soil in the region where the earliest contacts between Gaulish immigrants and Greek traders took place. Mastramele is a well-preserved Greek city on the Mediterranean coast west of Marseilles, of unique importance. The later town of Ugium shows traces of early Christian times; in the neighbourhood are also signs of neolithic settlement as well as medieval monuments. Long and continuous occupation.

64 Celto-Hellenic Lion, the Lion de L'Arcoule, at Le Baux (Bouches-du-Rhône). A model of Greek-influenced Celtic sculpture, associated with other remains less well peserved and more fragmentary, third century B.C. Traces back to oriental prototypes. Two main fragments. Forepart of animal in picture. Native limestone. Height overall 1 m. 10, width at mane 63 cm., depth at head 55 cm. Sitting rear part 48 cm. high, 60 cm. broad, 43 cm. deep. Musée Reattu, Arles.

Romanization of the Lower Rhône Valley

65 & 66 Excavations at Glanum (Bouches-du-Rhône). On the northern slope of the Alpilles, above St-Remy, the remains of a town—about one-tenth up to now—have been excavated since 1921. According to H. Rolland, the present Director of Excavations, there are four distinct levels of occupation. The oldest goes back to pre-classical Celtic times. An aboriginal shrine with headstones that have been used again shows analogies with Entremont and Roquepertuse. Parts are of Hellenistic date, recognizable by large blocks of squared-masonry in walls of typical Greek workmanship (2nd century B.C.). But most of the houses are of the Roman period, the first half of the first century B.C., rebuilt during the lively housing activity that took place under the Romans in the second half of that century and went on into the last third of the third century A.D. Some have been altered several times. But both the later phases have left traces of their influence, so that in Glanum—the Greek Glanon—we can trace the progress of architecture over half a millennium and compare the successive techniques in examples side by side. In the foreground of 65 is a peristyle (hall of pillars) surrounding an impluvium (basin for rainwater catchment) in a house of Hellenistic date (Maison des Antes). Beyond it the excavations to the south. 66 shows, stretching down to the north-west and St-Remy the entire quarter, partly rebuilt, consisting mainly of Hellenistic houses. Glanum was destroyed in A.D. 270 by German attacks.

67 Early Pillar Construction in Glanum. This example shows by means of a photograph taken some decades ago the former state of things, since excavated fragments and modern restorations were combined into complete pillars regardless of context, while in the foreground of 65, on the right, the present, much more cautious presentation of the same pillars can be seen, only preserving the genuine Ionic parts, thus allowing a comparison.

68 Upper Part of a Grooved Buttress in Glanum. The architectural context of this pillar with its Corinthian capital can be seen in 66. (Both photographs show state in 1958.)

69–70 Mosaic of Net and Dolphin, at Glanum. Hellenistic work in the House of the Ibex, so called after mosaics on its floor representing this among other animals, ranking as the oldest mosaic found in Gaul so far. Underneath the stone flags in the oiling-room (unctorium) of the Roman baths (thermae), this floor was laid out in sixteen squares and a centre-piece overlapping the innermost squares. Four dolphins at each corner and in the centre-piece. Ibex head in centre. The net and the dolphins form part of the original decorative elements of Mediterranean art. First century B.C. Height 3 m. 94, breadth 3 m. 76. Outside dolphins (69) 36½ cm. high, 85 cm. long.

71 Steps Down to Basin of Nymphaeum, at Glanum. The Nymphaeum, erected over a well already sacred in Celtic times, was restored by Agrippa, son-in-law to Augustus, in 20 B.C. as part of the foundation of the Temple of Valetudo (Goddess of Health). Altars and votive steles behind it. Left, remains of a shrine of Hercules. The wall in the left background supported the native Celtic shrine.

72 Fasciform Corner-ornament (Akroterion), at Glanum. The knot in the binding represents a type commonly used by sailors on cables, etc., in antiquity. Height 86 cm., breadth to right 69 cm., to left 55 cm. Height of ornament alone 77 cm.

73 Hypocaust of the Roman Baths, at Glanum. Pillars made of rectangular tiles support the oblong 'suspensura' tiles which carried the floor of terrazzo (conglomerate filled with crushed slate) in the hot room (calidarium). The external furnace room warmed air which flowed under the floor and up pipes in the walls. Pillars 70 cm. high at intervals of 38 cm. Section of pillars 21 cm. square.

74 Decorated Cornice, at Glanum. Vegetation motif surmounted by lion's head resting on a bracket. Such heads, stylized almost to the point of squareness, are a favourite ornament for the upper exterior of Roman houses. Native stone 46 cm. high. Width of fragment 75 cm., depth 106 cm. Lion's head 25 cm. high, 28 cm. broad. Profile of ornament projects 35 cm. from face of wall.

75 Town Gate of Glanum. The oldest town gate that has been preserved in Gaul, it stood across the north entrance. Picture shows the inner side. Left and right of the arch, between pillars, captive Gauls, symbolizing the conquest of the country by Caesar. The archivolt bears rich ornamentation of native fruits. Left and right, above, hovering genii of victory. The embayed ceiling in the vault of the gateway is very well preserved. About 40 B.C. Height of remains 8 m. 60, height under vaulting 7½ m., length 12 m. 40, breadth 5m. 60.

76 Cenotaph of the Grandson of Augustus, outside Glanum. Unusually well-preserved Roman monument; being a memorial to the dead it had to stand outside the city precincts. It commemorates Caius, called 'the Prince of Youth' who died in A.D. 4, and Lucius, killed in action at the age of 19, Erected about A.D. 10. Two square lower tiers with open arcades at the top, and a round third tier of twelve Corinthian columns, covered with a cupola, under which stand the statues of the two young men. Frieze above the four fluted Corinthian corner pilasters of the middle tier with battle scenes on hellenistic model, mythological motifs in some way relevant to the dead. H. Rolland has shown by analogies with coins that this is indeed the grandson of Augustus, to whom a temple at Nîmes (115) was also dedicated. Height 19 m. 30. Plinth 6½ m. long.

77 & 78 Roman Theatre, at Arles. Built under Augustus, the theatre at Colonia Julia Paterna Arelate Sextanorum, to give it its full name, stood on the plain and not, as at Vienne, Vaison, and Orange, on the side of a hill. The rows of seats were supported on arcades over vaulted corridors and were originally much higher. In 77 we see the deep slot, still in a good state of repair, into which the curtain sank, with behind it part of the wall of the arcade, converted into a fortified tower in the Middle Ages. The two Corinthian columns in 78 are made of African and Italian marble, remains of the once magnificent interior fittings. Axis of stage 104 m. long.

79 Centaur from Theatre, at Orange (Vaucluse). Fragment of frieze from interior of Augustan theatre. Marble 41 cm. high, 36½ cm. long, width of slab 16½ cm. Fragment of centaur 24 cm. high, 32½ cm. long, depth of relief 4.2 cm. Municipal Museum, Orange.

80 Charioteer Cupid, from Arles. This fragment found in the Roman theatre, is part of a rounded frieze, decorated with similar motifs, perhaps designed for the circus. Native stone, 35 cm. high, 55 cm. long, depth of stone 43 cm. From the Pagan Lapidarium, Arles.

81 Winged Goddess of Victory, from Arles. This fragment of a flat Hellenistic relief, depicting a victory beside a fluted pilaster, was probably part of the decoration of a triumphal arch, even though it was found in the theatre. Early first century A.D. Native stone. Height 2 m. 20, length 1 m. 30. Fragment of figure 1 m. 55, 85 cm. broad, that is slightly larger than life-size.

82 & 83 Two Dancing Girls, from Arles. Both figures, imitated from Greek models, formed part of the decoration of the Roman theatre where they were found. First century A.D. marble. Height of 82, 1 m. 44, width 65 cm., depth 34 cm. Height of 83, 1 m. 50, breadth 65 cm., depth 42 cm. Pagan Lapidarium, Arles.

84 Lady with Freedwoman, Arles. Example of a funeral tablet dedicated to her departed mistress by manumitted servant, as is evident from the inscription below the relief. Native stone. What is left of the stele measures 1 m. 17 in height, 46 cm. in breadth, 42 cm. in depth. Busts 50 cm. high, 45 cm. broad. Pagan Lapidarium, Arles.

85 & 86 The Roman Amphitheatre, Arles. Dating from the first third of the second century A.D., probably built under Hadrian (formerly ascribed to the first century), renovated in the fourth century as an inscription records. The largest surviving amphitheatre in Gaul, called locally 'les Arenes.' Probably had a seating capacity of 26,000; the rows of seats cover 12,000 square metres. Linear axis 136 m., lateral axis 107 m. Every tier has 60 arcades. The uppermost row of seats that remain are shown in 85, also the construction of the arcades in the top tier. (There is no Attica, in contrast to Nîmes.) In centre, exit from the vomitorium. The tower above the upper story dates from the twelfth century when the amphitheatre was used as a fort. Outermost gangway on ground floor shown in 86. These are not vaulted, as at Nîmes, but covered with slabs, more in the Greek tradition.

87 Apse of Roman Baths, at Arles. Called, from the palatial appearance of the building, 'Palais de la Trouille,' the municipal baths are preserved in several parts: the Caldarium is in a specially intact state, and the apse seen here opens into it. Other parts have been built over in *opus mixtum* (alternate courses of brick and masonry), a typical Roman building technique. Era of Constantine.

88 Aqueduct at Barbegal (Bouches-du-Rhône). Eastward of Arles, at the foot of the Alpilles, are to be seen the remains of a highly developed Roman water system which brought potable spring water from a little range of hills into Arles. Above the broken arch on the right is the actual water channel, thickly lined with cement.

89 Battery of Water-mills at Barbegal. A second aqueduct, parallel with that in 88, led through a tunnel in the rock to a series of Gallo-Roman water-mills. There were sixteen of them, arranged in pairs, on the south slope from the hill, driven by eight graduated falls of the same mill-leat. This is seen in the centre of the picture, with the mills on either side. Stairway beside leat. Fourth century A.D.

90 Pons Julius. Roman Bridge West of Apt (Arta Julia) over the Calavon (Vaucluse). The best-preserved Roman road-bridge in Gaul, still carrying traffic to Bonnieux today. Three wide arches carried on four piers span the river. The two middle piers are pierced by vaulted channels to relieve pressure of flood waters. First century A.D. Height at centre 14 m. Length 70 m. Width 4½ m.

91 Small Roman Bridge near Cereste, over the Encreme (Basses-Alpes). This little town, a Roman foundation near the Via Domitia which as early as pre-Roman times was an important traffic-link between the Alps and the Rhône, was served by two small Roman bridges. The other one was over Aiguebelle. Restored as to the upper part, the bearing arch and flood-channels on the left have been untouched since Roman times.

92 Veiled Woman. Fragment of relief from pagan sarcophagus of first century A.D. Marble. 33 cm. high. Forehead 19 cm. broad. Depth 7 cm. Musée Borely, Marseilles.

93 Portrait Bust of a Boy. Probably a member of Octavian's family. Marble. 45 cm. high, breadth across shoulders 41 cm. Depth 31 cm. Head measures 24 cm. high, 23 cm. wide, 25 cm. deep. Pagan Lapidarium, Arles.

94 Portrait Bust of Massiliot Magistrate. Apparently copied from a waxen death-mask. From the cemetery called 'du Lazaret.' Julian or Claudian period. Carrara marble, 37 cm. high, breadth of forehead 19 cm., depth 23 cm. Musée Borely, Marseilles.

95 GABLE OF SARCOPHAGUS LID WITH MYTHOLOGICAL SCENES. On tympanum (centre): Medea, wife of Jason, preparing to slay her children. On the acroteries (left): Odysseus, recognized by his nurse by his scars, silencing her. His dog under his foot. (Right) Œdipus and the sphinx. Second or third century A.D. Marble 90 cm. high, 1 m. 57 broad. Musée Borely, Marseilles.

96 HUNTING SCENE FROM SARCOPHAGUS. The left side of this tomb showed a boar hunt. This, the right half, shows men hunting red deer with nets, no doubt in co-operation with hounds as in 191 below, The mounted huntsman wears a hood like the horse-dealer in 207 below.

97 & 98 MYTHOLOGICAL SCENES, FROM SARCOPHAGUS. Showing departure of Hippolytus, setting out for the hunt, the hunt itself (97) and the death of Hippolytus (98). Found near Trinquetaille, right bank of Rhône in the Camargue Delta. Note similarity of motif with 96. Second or third century. Marble. Height 99 cm., length of whole sarcophagus 2 m. 35, breadth 94–99 cm. Pagan Lapidarium, Arles.

99 PONT DU GARD AQUEDUCT. Erected in 19 B.C. on the orders of Augustus's stepson Agrippa, to carry water from the spring at Eure, near Uzés, across the bed of the River Gard or Gardon, 30 miles to Nîmes. Three tiers: the first 22 m. high, six arches; the second 19 m. high, 242 m. long, eleven arches; the third, 7 m. high, 275 m. long, thirty-five arches. The section shown here contains the central arch which is somewhat longer than the others, carrying four spans of the upper tier instead of the more usual three. A road bridge was built downstream and alongside the lowest tier in the eighteenth century. The water channel on top of the uppermost tier is 1 m. 45 deep and 1 m. 22 broad, covered with flags some of which are still in place.

100 FAÇADE WALL OF ROMAN THEATRE AT ORANGE (Vaucluse). Outer face of the wall closing the stage area from the rear, the only one that has survived intact. Monumental centre entrance below and nine doors on either side. Above, a double row of 43 socket stones, which held the poles supporting the *velum* (awning). Twenty-one blind arcades below. Built under Augustus. Height 36 m. 82, length 103 m. 15.

101 & 102 TROPHIES ON TRIUMPHAL ARCH AT ORANGE. This arch, one of the most important in Gaul, had three gateways and is a war memorial, commemorating the victory of the XVIth Legion called Gallica over the forces of the Gaulish chieftains Mario, Udilles, Dacurda, and Avot whose names have been chiselled on the shields of the prisoners depicted on the east front. Half a century later the successors of the Augustan legionaries re-dedicated the monument to Tiberius, which has given rise to a false dating. Overall dimensions 18m. 80 high, 19 m. 50 broad, 8 m. 50 deep. 101 shows the trophies of the victory by land. 102 the spoils of the sea-fight against Marseilles, together illustrating both the weapons of Gallic troops and Greek naval armament, including parts of warships.

103 MANACLED PRISONERS ON TRIUMPHAL ARCH AT CARPENTRAS (Vaucluse). At the entrance to the Gallo-Roman town of Carpentoracte stood a triumphal arch that was later adapted to serve as the porch of the first cathedral, a Romanesque building. Grooved pillars supported the single vaulted passage. All parts higher than the archivolt have been destroyed. Figures of prisoners chained to monument are well preserved and provide interesting detail of clothing and weapons of lower Rhône barbarians, both Celtic and Germanic, in the first half-century A.D. Height 10 m., width 5 m. 90, depth 4 m. 54. In rear courtyard of Palais de Justice, Carpentras.

104–6 THREE PORTRAITS OF THE WINDS AT SISTERON (Basses-Alpes). These came to light in the course of excavations for a new hospital. There were also fragments of statues of the Muses, comic and tragic masks, etc., and are thought to be parts of the decoration-acroteria—of a monumental mausoleum in the town which in Roman times was called Segustero. 104 is 62 cm. high, 30 cm. broad, 35 cm. deep. 105 is 45 cm. high, 35 cm. deep. 106 is 55 cm. high, 36 cm. broad, 28 cm. deep. A fourth wind, badly mutilated, is 45 cm. high, 34 cm. broad, 25 cm. deep.

107 FOUR CORINTHIAN COLUMNS WITH ARCHITRAVE AT RIEZ (Basses-Alpes). These are remains of a Roman temple at the Gallo-Roman town at Reiz. The columns are of grey granite. Architrave and bases of white marble. Bases 40 cm. high, on square plinths 30 cm. high and 1 m. 15 square. Circumference of pillars is the same as the distance between them—2 m. 28.

108 EXCAVATIONS AT VAISON-LA-ROMAINE (Vaucluse). Vasio Vocontiorum, a considerable Celtic town, became in the course of Romanization the richest town in the area of the left bank of the Rhône. Excavations there, directed by the late Canon J. Sautel and under the generous patronage of M. Burrus, have revealed not only isolated buildings (a theatre, a basilica, baths, and bridges) but many quarters of the town on the slopes of the Puymin hill and is the lower suburb of La Villasse, with many well-preserved private houses and whole stretches of road surface. Vaison bears the clearest imprint of Roman urbanization on Gallic soil. This is a general view of the La Villasse quarter. The arcade in the centre belongs to the basilica in the foreground. Behind that the Romanesque cathedral, built on the site of an early Christian basilica; pieces of columns from Vasio were used as the foundations of a Merovingian apse.

109 HEAD OF VENUS WREATHED IN LAUREL, FROM VAISON. Head of a statue, found in 1924 in the peristyle of the House of the Mesii (Puymin). First or second century A.D. White marble 28 cm. high, 24 cm. broad, 26 cm. deep. From Vaison Museum.

110 OLD SATYR, FROM VAISON. One face of a Janus-type double head. The other face was that of Bacchus. First or second century A.D. Marble, 23 cm. high, 16 cm broad, depth to junction with reverse face 15 cm Vaison Museum

111 HEAD OF GIRL, FROM ALAUNIUM (Basses-Alpes). About 3 km. east of Forcalquier, found on the site of still incompletely excavated Gallo-Roman town. Limestone, 11 cm. high, 8 cm. broad, depth including hair 11 cm. Forcalquier Museum.

112 HEAD OF A MAN, FROM VIENNE (Isère). First or second century A.D. Native stone, 30 cm. high, 22 cm. broad, 29 cm. deep. Lapidarium of St-Pierre, Vienne.

113 RUINS OF A COUNTRY TEMPLE NEAR VERNEGUES (Bouches-du-Rhône). All that remains of this shrine, built on a hillside, are the foundations, the left inner wall of the *cella* as illustrated here, with a square built-in buttress, and a fluted Corinthian column from the vestibule. Proportions and sculpture of the capitals mark it as a work of great beauty. First century A.D. (Compare 259.)

114 PART OF TEMPLE BUILT OVER SACRED SPRING, AT NÎMES (Gard). Known as 'The Temple of Diana' this building whose vaulted ceiling has fallen in is a main hall in relation to the Nymphaeum. Some have seen in it part of a public bath-house. It is a *cella* of rectangular shape. The square space in the middle may have been intended for the statue of a god. To left and right of it there are further square chambers, marked off by apses. In the side walls and the inner face of the façade which was pierced by three doors there were twelve niches, preserved on the right-hand side. Fragments of fallen ceiling decoration found in all the rooms. Probably built in the reign of Hadrian, first third of the second century A.D.

115 ROMAN TEMPLE, KNOWN AS THE MAISON CARRÉE, AT NÎMES. Built in the reign of Agrippa, son-in-law of Augustus, on the Greek model, it was dedicated at the beginning of the first century A.D. to his sons, the grandsons of Augustus, Caius and Lucius (see 76). Fifteen steps lead up to the portico:

formerly there were more. The *cella* consists of a single rectangular oblong chamber with twenty Corinthian columns, free-standing. The columns are 7 m. 35 high, with capitals 1 m. 03, the architrave and frieze together 2m. 40. Height of main gateway (originally the source of light) 6 m. 83, width 3 m. 28. The original roof did not resemble the present one which is a nineteenth-century restoration. The *cella* is now used as a museum of Roman sculpture.

116 & 117 AMPHITHEATRE AT NÎMES. Somewhat smaller than the sister-building at Arles (85 & 86) and called, like it, Les Arenes; this one must have been built in the first century A.D. and offered seating for 24,000 spectators in 34 rows. Elliptical in shape, made of stone from Barutel, which is 7 km. north-west of Nîmes, it is 21 m. high, 133 m. long, 101 m. wide. 116 shows the two tiers of arcade with remains of the story (attica) which is only partly preserved, left, above. Arcades divided on ground floor, by pilasters, on upper floor by walled-in Doric pillars with bases. The attica had 120 projecting stone brackets with holes to take the poles of the velum. The masonry was 33 m. thick from the outer to the inner walls. 117 shows typical Roman vaulting of corridor between rows of seats.

118 & 119 BOUCRANIA, FROM NÎMES. Two friezes with human heads and the skulls of oxen in wreaths of flowers. These beribboned animal skulls in conjunction with sun-symbols typify sacrifice. They are part of the decorations of the amphitheatre. Native stone. 118 is 57 cm. high, 1 m. long, 25 cm. deep. Diameter of wreath 41 cm. Head 13 cm. high, 13 cm. broad. Depth of relief 5 cm. Wreath adjoining skull protrudes 6½ cm. from surface of stone. Ox skulls including horns 41 cm. high, 39 cm. broad. 119, 56 cm. high, 1 m. 19 long, 30 cm. deep. Skull 44 cm. high, 37 cm. broad. Diameter of wreath 38 cm. Head 15 cm. high, 14 cm. broad, depth of relief 6 cm. Skull and wreath protrude 7 cm. Archaeological Museum, Nîmes.

120 FRIEZE OF EAGLES, FROM ARLES. The eagle with its right wing folded and left wing extended in relief, holds in its beak one end of a garland of leaves and flowers. Found on the southern fortified wall of Arelate. Native stone, 16 cm. high, 1 m. 57 long, 82 cm. deep. Similar fragments of friezes with eagles were found in the theatre and in the cryptoporticus. Pagan Lapidarium, Arles.

121 HEAD OF APOLLO, FROM NÎMES. Fragment of a bronze statue, larger than life-size, found at the fountain called Nemausus. Almost certainly representing Apollo. Height 41 cm., breadth 22 cm., height of face alone 26 cm. Maison Carrée, Nîmes.

122 HEAD OF VENUS, FROM NÎMES. Roman copy of Greek prototype. Marble. Height 38½ cm., breadth 22 cm., depth 27 cm. Face alone 18 cm. high. Maison Carrée, Nîmes.

123 HEAD OF A PRINCE, PROBABLY ONE OF THE FAMILY OF AUGUSTUS, FROM VAISON (Vaucluse). First century. Black granite. Height 22 cm., breadth 18 cm., depth 20 cm. Lapidarium Calvet, Avignon.

124 PORTRAIT OF THE EMPEROR TRAJAN WHO LIVED FROM A.D. 57 TO 117 AND REIGNED FROM A.D. 98 TO 117, FROM CARPENTRAS (Vaucluse). Very lightly waved hair combed forward on to the forehead. The expression of the face, especially the lively modelling of the area round the mouth, is very characteristic of Roman portraiture early in the second century A.D. Marble, 22 cm. high, 20 cm. broad, 19 cm. deep. Lapidarium Calvet, Nîmes.

125 STELE OF T. TESSICNIUS SECUNDUS AND HIS WIFE JULIA FROM MONS (Gard). Found in the ruins of Vieilla Cionta, commune of Mons, this funerary tablet to a married couple consists of an arcade surmounting two busts, with above it a decorative motif of leaves and flowers spreading out on both sides with a dolphin in each corner. The orthography, with double-S in the name Tessicnius indicates a pronunciation like English th, common in Celtic names and sometimes written Ɖ, as in Ɖirone for Sirona. The name of the potter Messilius at Vienne is spelt in the same way as here. Native stone. Height of whole stele 1 m. 32, breadth 75 cm., depth 25 cm., height of letters 5.6 cm. Lapidarium Calvet, Vaucluse.

Rome, The World Power

126 Temple of Augustus and Livia, at Vienne (Isere). Apart from the Maison Carrée at Nîmes this is the only Roman temple in Gaul that is completely preserved; it is in even better state than the one at Nîmes. Built at the opening of the first century A.D., it was originally dedicated to the honour of Rome and of the emperor; but after the death of Augustus and of his consort Livia it was re-dedicated to the Imperial couple as patron deities of the Imperial family. Six fluted Corinthian columns in the façade and five at each side carry the roof and enclose the narrow rectangular *cella* with a porch and transcepts, 17 m. high, 14½ m. wide, and 24 m. long. The roof is better and more completely preserved than that of the Maison Carrée at Nîmes (115); Vienne was the capital of the Allobrogi whose territory extended from Grenoble to Geneva, and in 46 B.C. under Julius Caesar became Colonia Julia, capital of one of the seventeen provinces of Gaul In the reign of Diocletian it became the headquarters for all of south-eastern Gaul, and was the base where the commander of the Rhône flotilla flew his flag.

127 Somnus (Hypnos), the God of Sleep, at Vienne. Here shown as a boy but recognisable by the little wings over his temples. The head seems to have touched the upper edge of the relief, which explains its being slightly inclined. Somnus appears frequently on tombstones and sarcophagi. First century A.D. Marble, 27 cm. high, 24 cm. broad, 14 cm. deep. Relief protrudes 10 cm. Lapidarium St-Pierre, Vienne.

128 Profile of Augustus, from Vienne. Gaius Julius Caesar Octavianus (63 B.C.-A.D. 14) was the first Roman Emperor. This fragment shows him as quite a young man still, wearing the crown of oak leaves which the Senate granted him in 27 B.C. with the title of Augustus 'ob cives servatos.' But he was in fact 36 at the time. Marble, 21 cm. high, 14 cm. wide. The head has been detached from the relief plaque of which it forms part. Lapidarium St-Pierre, Vienne.

129 Bust of a Bearded God, from Vienne. Fragment of relief, probably Neptune or Jupiter. Torso frontally presented with head in left profile, 36 cm. high, 38 cm. wide, 18½ cm. deep. Relief stands out 14 cm. (The whole of the left shoulder is in fact shown.)

130 Bust of Attis with Phrygian Cap, from Vienne. Wearing a mantle with long sleeves and fastened on the right shoulder. He has raised his right hand with the index finger bent back, a characteristic attitude in pictures commemorating manumission. Second half of first century A.D. Limestone Height 52 cm., breadth of whole stone 1 m. 10, depth 40 cm. Relief protrudes 18 cm. The entire figure of the god extended over three blocks of stone and must therefore have stood 1 m. 56 high Lapidarium St-Pierre, Vienne.

131 Leopardess and Bowl of Fruit in 'Pulpitum' of Theatre, at Vienne. Part of the decorations of the Roman theatre preserved *in situ*. Carrara marble. Height 23½ cm., length 44 cm., depth 9 cm. Leopard alone 15 cm. high, 21 cm. long: relief stands out 3 cm. Bowl alone: height 11 cm. × 11 broad, relief 3½ cm.

132 Molossian Hound in 'Pulpitum' of Theatre, at Vienne. Part of the same frieze as 131. Dog in crouching attitude preparing to attack, looking upwards with open mouth. The ears point backwards, the hackles are raised. The breed of mastiffs is often mentioned in Classical poetry. Carrara marble, 23½ cm. high, 45 cm. long, 10 cm. deep. Dog 34 cm. long, relief 3 cm.

133 Mosaic of Orpheus, at Vienne. Hexagonal central mosaic with figure of the god with his lyre: animals under his spell grouped round it in medallions: boar, horse, etc. Orpheus sits in a niche of the rocks. The lyre with seven strings is held on his left knee and played with the right hand while the left holds the instrument. Examples from the colour scheme are: cloak green with blue outer cloak; hair brown; headdress green and red. Height 91 cm., breadth 93 cm. Lapidarium St-Pierre, Vienne.

134 LIONS ON THE 'PULPITUM' OF THE THEATRE, AT VIENNE. This fragment of a frieze shows the animals converging on the central niche of the front wall of the stage from right and left. Part of the upper border of the frieze can be seen above the head of the lion on the left. Carrara marble, 25 cm. high, 50 cm. long, 13 cm. deep. The lion in the centre is 16 cm. high and 31 cm. long.

135 MOSAIC OF LEAPING LEOPARDS, VIENNE. The colour scheme is black and a greenish yellow. Whole mosaic 80 cm. square. Figure of leopard 41 cm. high × 73 cm., nose to tail tip. Lapidarium St-Pierre, Vienne.

136 MITHRAIC SATURN-STATUE, FROM ARLES. The figure of the god, wreathed in serpents, originally had the head of a lion, which has been broken off, but traces of the mane remain on the neck, signs of the Zodiac between the coils of the snake: TAURUS ARIES GEMINE above CANCER LEO VIRGO in centre LIBRAE SCORPIO SAGITTARIUS below. The nethermost file of three is missing. Mithras was the Iranian god of light whose cult spread to the City of Rome via Greece and became widespread in the western provinces of the Empire from the end of the first century A.D. onwards. It reached its zenith towards the end of the third century. This marble statue was found in the Roman circus. Height of remaining fragment 1 m., breadth of shoulders and snake 46 cm., depth including snake 34 cm. Pagan Lapidarium, Arles.

137 CROWNED HEAD OF A WOMAN, FROM VIENNE. Doubtless a personification of Colonia Julia Vienna. Typical hair style of first century underneath the diadem. Bronze. Height 30 cm., breadth 21 cm., depth including hair knots 24 cm. Lyons Museum.

138 MOSAIC: BATTLE OF HERCULES AND ANTAEUS, FROM AVENTICUM (Canton de Vaud). The artist seized the moment when Hercules raises Antaeus off the ground, to prevent him renewing his strength by contact with Gaea. Otherwise it would serve, technically, to illustrate the Roman style of wrestling. This was part of a large mosaic of which only the centre remains in good condition. Height 1 m. 17. Found at Conches-dessus, near Avenches. Roman Museum, Avenches (Switzerland).

139 HUNTING SCENE, FROM THE MOSAIC OF BOSCEAZ (Canton de Vaud). Detail from the right-hand border of the great mosaic of the gods. A huntsman with a spear holds a cheetah on a double leash. They are on the track of a boar, together with other cheetahs further to the left. Near Orbe (Switzerland).

140 DETAIL OF CIRCUS MOSAIC, AT LYONS. The scene depicts an obstacle race for quadrigae, with two youths holding a laurel wreath and palm branch in the middle of the double-wall jump, and a single rider. The latter is probably a judge or some other racecourse official, as similar figures appear in the racecourse mosaic from Horkstow in Lincolnshire and in the terracotta racecourse moulding now in the British Museum. The pyramidal object is the 'metal' or post marking the end of the lap at either end of the 'spina' or low wall which ran down the centre of the arena making an oval track. The whole picture was framed in a wide garland and shows other scenes from the circus also. Overall dimensions 1 m. 30 high, 3 m. 15 long. Found in the Ainay quarter of Lyons, between the Saone and the Rhône.

141 SHE-WOLF SUCKLING ROMULUS AND REMUS, FROM AVENTICUM. This block was at the top of a fair-sized monument. Its other side was sloping and was chiselled to represent the tiled roof of a sheep-fold. Here the she-wolf of Rome is shown in a shallow den between two trees, with the twins. Bird's nest in branches on left. Local limestone, 58 cm. high, 111 cm. long. depth between 54 and 44 cm. Relief stands out 10 cm. Avenches Museum, Switzerland.

142 Head of a God Crowned with Flowers, from Vienne. Mosaic. Height 52½ cm., breadth 49 cm. Musée St-Pierre, Vienne.

143 Bust of Marcus Aurelius (Lived A.D. 121–180), at Aventicum. Wearing the *lorica squameata* or scale-cuirass, the *paludamentum* or general's cloak thrown over the left shoulder, with a winged gorgoneion on the chest. The bust is beaten out of a single 22-carat gold plate. Height 33.54 cm., breadth 29.46 cm., weight 1 k. 598. The bust has also been ascribed to Antoninus Pius who lived from A.D. 86 to 161 and reigned from A.D. 138 to 161. Marcus Aurelius Antoninus was his foster-son.

144 Bust of Woman, from Allmendingen near Thun (Canton Berne). Probably represents the Celtic goddess Rosmerta Maia in Gallo-Roman guise of which the hairstyle is a typical feature. Second century A.D. Bronze, 13 cm. high, 8 cm. wide. Historical Museum, Berne.

145 Head of Helvetian, from Prilly (Canton Vaud). According to R. Laur-Belart, 'The attitude and expression of the head show clearly that the subject belongs to the Celtic population of Switzerland,' but the technique is that of a Roman artist. Bronze with copper eyes. Height 27½ cm., breadth 19½ cm., depth 20 cm. Historical Museum, Berne.

146–50 Five Details from the Mosaic of Gods, at Bosceaz (Canton Vaud). Of thirteen octagonal medallions, arranged in pairs or threes, the seven innermost ones portray the gods who gave their names to the Roman days of the week. 146, Sol with his four-horse chariot (*quadriga*). 149, Luna or Cynthia the moon-goddess in her pair-horse chariot or *biga*. 147, Venus in the centre; Friday is still named after her in French and Italian, *Vendredi*, *Venerdi*. The other six figures are marine deities (148 and 150) together with Narcissus and Ganymede. The border shows scenes of animal life and hunting (compare 139). Diameter of each medallion 67½ cm. Site is near Orbe in Switzerland.

151 Head of Lion Vertillum (Côte d'Or). The mane is remarkable for the way it grows up out of the stone, framing the lion's face like an ornament. Found at Vertault, the Gallo-Roman Vertillum. Local stone, 65 cm. high, including 10 cm. plinth, 40 cm. wide, 26 cm. deep. Archaeological Museum, Dijon.

152 Eagle, from Malain (Côte d'Or). Fragment of a cornice, at the angle of which two eagles were carved. Overall measurements: 34 cm. high, 1 m. long, 62 cm. deep. Fragment of eagle measures 19 cm. high, breadth across wings 17 cm., relief 2½ cm. Archaeological Museum, Dijon.

153 Temple of Janus, near Autun (Saone-et-Loire). The building was square and stood just outside the modern town, though well within the limits of the Galo-Roman Augustodunum. It is an example of how, throughout the Empire, sacred buildings assumed regional forms. Here the *cella* is round or polygonal inside a rectangular outer precinct, like the Tour de Vésone at Périgueux for instance. There is no proof of the dedication to Janus: the masonry is of Roman type, with built-in arcades. Height 24 m., ground plan 16½ m. square.

154 Bearded Hercules, from Dijon. One face of four-sided block of stone supporting a column. Overall measurements 97 cm. high, 62½ cm. wide, 47 cm. deep. Head alone 19 cm. high, 14½ cm. broad. Relief stands out 5½ cm. Found at Tour du Petit St-Benigne. Archaeological Museum, Dijon.

155 Head of Juno, from Alesia. The goddess, whose features are so full as almost to be described as heavy, wears a diadem, bowed in front, over her hair which has been drawn smoothly back to form a bun at the nape. Bronze, 9 cm. high, 8½ cm. wide, 12 cm. deep, including hair-bun. Alesia Museum, Alise-Ste-Reine.

156 Arch of Germanicus at Saintes (Charente-Maritime). The inscription records that Caius Rufus, a Gaul, built this double arch in honour of Tiberius, his younger brother Germanicus, and his son Drusus. The arch with its twelve fluted Corinthian columns originally stood in the middle of the Roman bridge across the Charente in the town of Mediolanum Santonum. It was re-erected on the right bank of the river during the nineteenth century. It is 13 m. high, 15 m. wide, and 3 m. thick.

157 GATE OF MARS AT REIMS. This is another triumphal arch, wrongly ascribed to the Augustan period, whereas it was not built until the beginning of the third century A.D. Of all the arches in Gaul it and the one at Orange are the two most important monuments. The central arch is somewhat higher than the side ones. On the vaulting of the passages there are mythological scenes such as Romulus and Remus and their foster-mother, and allegories of the months. Height 13½ m., width 33 m., depth 6m.

158 COLD ROOM (FRIGIDARIUM) OF THE ROMAN BATHS AT LUTETIA PARISIORUM. This monumental building stood midway between the courses of the modern Boulevards St-Michel and St-Germain. Its rooms were very large and this one, the main hall with steps leading down into the cold bath (left), has its vaulted roof intact. Its dimensions give a clear picture of the Roman style in municipal buildings of this kind. Height 14½ m., length 31 m., width 12 m. At the crest of the vault the roof is 65 cm. thick, the walls 2 m. thick in places. Early third century A.D. reigns of Septimus or Caracalla. Now Lapidarium for Musée Cluny.

159 APOLLO, FROM LA COURIÈRE (Creuse). This bronze statue, found in the region of Bourganeuf, a masterpiece of Roman-Gallic sculpture, is unfortunately mutilated about the hands. The right leg from the knee downwards and the left foot are missing. Natural size. Louvre, Paris.

160 DEATH-MASK OF A ROMAN LEGIONARY. Sepulchral mask from the Chassenard cremation-grave, used in conjunction with a visored helmet. The cast must have been taken after death, to judge by the slit-like eyes and the slightly open mouth. It was found with the remains of a suit of armour which had been fused by cremation; part of this can be seen above the forehead. Wrought iron. 17½ cm. high, 26 cm. wide from ear to ear, 15 cm. deep. Antiquités Nationales.

161 HEAD OF APOLLO, FROM LILLEBONNE. This Norman town was named Juliobona after Julius Caesar. Since four images of Apollo were found there, this god is regarded as the patron of Lillebonne. The head here illustrated is a good example of Roman bronze work, as practised throughout Gaul. Second or third century. Natural size. Departmental Museum, Rouen.

162 BULL, FROM LILLEBONNE WITH SLIGHTLY RAISED FOREFOOT. Remarkable for the taut, severe treatment of head and body; whereas the feet are modelled in great detail, the bulk of the figure is treated as one mass. Bronze, 20 cm. high, 31 cm. long, 8 cm. wide. Departmental Museum, Rouen.

163 RELIEF OF ABRAXAS, FROM NYON (Canton Vaud). Together with other oriental cults, that of Abraxas was brought to Gaul by the Roman legions. Two images of this god in avian form are known from Switzerland. A bronze applique now in the Archaeological Museum at Lausanne shows the god with human body, shield, and staff, legs like serpents, and the characteristic cock's head. The marble relief (also from the Lake of Geneva) shows him as a cock with curled tail, at the end of which the serpent's head left of the break is still just visible. Height 11 cm., breadth 13½ cm., depth 4½ cm. Historical Museum, Berne.

164 FRAGMENT OF RELIEF, FROM TRIER, WITH BATTLE SCENE. This work, full of dramatic movement, shows how the Romans, in sculpture throughout their empire, often commemorated their military conquests, in the guise of mythological scenes; on the left, naked barbarians; on the right a rearing charger with part of shield-bearing Roman cavalryman. First or second century A.D. Native stone, 88 cm. high, 1 m. 37 broad, relief stands out 11 cm. Rheinisches Landesmuseum, Trier.

165 Apse of the Imperial Baths, Trier. Next to the Baths of Caracalla and those of Diocletian in Rome itself, this is the biggest thermal establishment that has been preserved, from the later period of the Empire. Building began early in the fourth century. At the eastern end of the *decumanus maximus*, as the Romans called the central axis of their barracks and of cities which were built to a uniform plan. These baths were never completed because Constantine moved the seat of government to Byzantium in 316, and not until the third quarter of the century were they converted into a palace under Valentinian I. The two-storied apse with its high arcade of windows forms one side of the tepidarium. The picture gives a clear impression of late Roman building technique. The bath-palace covers an area of 260 m. × 145, and the walls still standing are up to 20 m. high.

166 North Gate of the Roman City of Trier, Called Porta Nigra. Originally a bright-coloured sandstone, only age and the grime of centuries earned it the name of the Black Gate, which it has borne since the twelfth century. The town was laid out in the reign of Augustus, and called after him Augusta Treverorum. In the fourth century it was surrounded with a fortified wall, when it had to serve as a bulwark in the system of defence against the invading Germans. The perimeter was 6½ km. and our picture shows the western tower and central part of the north gateway. There were two stories over the dual entrance and three in the towers, with 144 round windows as originally built. Height of west tower 29 m. 33, depth 21 m. 47, breadth of whole structure 36 m.

167 Roman Wall Painting, from Trier, Showing a Villa in the Land of the Treveri. This mural was found in the Palace Square at Trier, and represents a substantial Roman country house, headquarters of an estate, typical of the agricultural properties which were as much a mark of Roman material civilization in Gaul as were the cities themselves; the same is true of Britain. It is one of the few well-preserved mural frescoes in Gaul. One metre high, 1 m. 75 broad. Dimensions of this detail 90 × 83 cm.

168 Colossal Statue of Mercury, from Puy-de-Jouer, St Goussaud (Creuse). This huge fragment is an example of Gallic portraiture of Roman deities in central Gaul where Celtic tradition exerted the strongest influence. Granite, more than life-size. The whole statue was 2 m. 60 high. Musée Gueret (Creuse). Puy-de-Jouer was originally Mons Jovis—the Hill of Jupiter.

169–70 Mars and Venus, from a Square Buttress in Paris. Besides the unmistakable male deities Mars (169) and Vulcan (170) in profile, the female figure is probably Venus who is connected with both in mythology. But confusingly she carries a torch here. Remains of veil over her hair; Mars wears a visored helmet as in 160, and a gorget on his breast. Pseudo-attic, typically Antonine style. Yellowish limestone, 1 m. high, 5 cm. deep. Reverse side worked flat. Partly restored on horizontal surfaces. Musée de Cluny, Paris.

New Faces in Gaul

All the work in this section, unless otherwise stated, belongs to the Gallo-Roman period. On account of the mixture of styles more accurate dating is uncertain and controversial; the older traditions are carried forward with some modification of outward form.

171 The Goddess Sirona of Hochscheid (Rhineland). This Celtic goddess of earth and springs appears in Roman garb, wearing a diadem. The snake twined round her right forearm and the bowl of eggs in her left hand, to which she is pointing her right hand and letting the snake stretch its head towards them, both bear witness to her indigenous character, which the location of the statue, at a holy well confirms. The stone was 169 cm. high (but the missing lower part was 45 cm.), 57 cm. broad, 45 cm. deep. Relief stands out 31 cm.—almost completely in the round. Rheinisches Landesmuseum, Trier.

172 Statue of Succellus, from Visp (Valais). Although the treatment of the head had been influenced by Roman statues of Jupiter, the clothes (smock and tight Celtic breeches) as well as the attitude of the hands from which the long wooden mallet has been lost and other attributes point to the Celtic father of the gods. He was always conceived as a powerful male figure, probably identical with Caesar's Dis Pater, and is here offering the life-giving water in a bowl or beaker. Height 27 cm. Breadth across arms 18 cm. Kunsthistorisches Museum, Geneva.

173 Relief of Esus, from Paris. Square block with two Roman gods, Jove and Vulcan, and two Celtic gods, Tarvos Trigaranos (the bull with three horns or three cranes) and Esus, one of the three principal Gallic male deities to whom according to Lucan enemies killed in battle were offered. But his figure reminds us rather of a divine woodman; the clearance of forest land was of vital economic importance for the Gauls, to make room for food-crops. Blueish sandstone. Height 107 cm., 75 cm. wide × 75 cm. deep. Relief without the frame 90 cm., breadth 60 cm., relief stands out 6 cm. Musée Cluny, Paris.

174 Relief of Esus on Votive Slab, from Trier. On the front of the partly destroyed monument Mercury and Rosmerta, with a money-coffer between them; on the left side a female figure; on the right side, pictured here, Esus still more unmistakably clad as a woodman in a short tunic. In the crown of the tree which he is felling, Tarvos Trigaranos, the bull with three cranes (see 173). Overall measurements 2 m. 20 x 91 cm. × 58 cm. This detail 1 m. 15 high, 58 cm. broad (depth of whole monument) Rheinisches Landesmuseum, Trier.

175 Relief of Cernunnos, from Paris. The horned god with human visage is depicted on the same sort of square block as Esus (173) but only the upper part of this one with the head has been preserved. The horns usually take the form of stags' antlers; in this case they are adorned with typical Celtic neck-rings (torcs); height 41 cm., breadth 60 cm. Musée Cluny, Paris.

176 Rosmerta and Mercury, Relief from Glanum. The Celtic Rosmerta carries in her left hand the cornucopia attribute of the Roman Fortuna and in the right the sieve which is peculiar to her. Mercury, with wings both on the head and on the feet, carries his purse in his right hand and his herald's wreathed staff (originally with two snakes) in his left. He is accompanied by a goat and a tortoise. Native stone, 47½ cm. high, 54 cm. wide, 9 cm. deep with relief 3 cm. deep. Museum at St Remy-de-Provence (Bouches-du-Rhône).

177 Relief of Cernunnos Between Apollo and Mercury, from Rheims (Marne). The Celtic god, originally horned, sits with his legs tucked under him, wearing a torc and accompanied by a stag and a bull, between the Roman gods Apollo (left) and Mercury (right). He carries a club over his left arm and on his left arm a hunting net or a beast's hide, falling down over the seat and representing a purse full of money to symbolize his wealth. The third of his familiar beasts is in the gable-shaped space above him: it is the earth-bound rat. Native stone, 1 m. 30 high, 1 m. 24 wide, 36 cm. deep. Relief 16 cm. deep. Rheims Museum.

178 The Bear-goddess Artio of Muri (Berne). The goddess is seated on the left, holding out a bowl of fruit to a bear which is approaching from the forest, symbolized by tree on right. On her left another vessel also filled with fruit stands on a square pillar. The name of the goddess is plain from the inscription on the plinth: Deae Artioni—Licinia Sabinilla. Second or third century A.D. Bronze, 20 cm. high, 29 cm. wide. Historisches Museum, Berne.

179 Epona Accompanied by Fabulous Beasts on Funeral Stele from Agassac (Haute Garonne) Local Celtic adaptation of standard pattern funeral stele with mounted nereid and marine monsters. The Classical nereid has been transformed into the

Celtic horse-breeder's goddess Epona, and dressed in Gallic clothing. She is sitting sideways on the horse, not riding side-saddle as we understand it nowadays, but as female equestrian figures are shown down to the sixteenth century, full-face to the beholder, her left rand resting on the horse's neck; note the fish-tailed bull and the geometrical ornaments in the corners. Fragment of stone relief with remains of inscription, 67 cm. high, 44 cm. wide to break, 14 cm. deep. In the Mairie at Agassac.

180 STATUE OF EPONA, FROM ALESIA. Here too the goddess is shown full-face, seated, with her left hand resting protectively on the head of a foal. This sculpture though of the Gallo-Roman period preserves the Celtic tradition in its form as well as in its content. Native stone, 31 cm. high, 21 cm. broad, 13 cm. deep. Musée Alesia, Alise-St-Reine (Côte d'Or).

181 RELIEF OF EPONA. FROM ALTBACHTAL (Rhineland). In this third treatment of the Epona theme both the goddess and the horse have been rendered in heavily Romanized style. She sits in the attitude of 179, the reins in her left hand, in Roman dress with Roman coiffure. Her right hand holds a shallow bowl of fruit. Sophistication extends to the mare, pacing in parade style with mane and tail dressed in a formal manner. Native stone, 42 cm. high, 28 cm. broad, 14½ cm. deep. Relief stands out 5 cm. Rheinisches Landesmuseum, Trier.

182 RELIEF OF SEATED GALLO-ROMAN PAIR OF DEITIES, SAINTES (Charente-Maritime). The seated goddess on the right with her cornucopia might be Rosmerta. Her male companion, seated on the ground with his legs folded under him, must from his attitude be a Celtic god, but we cannot tell for certain which one since the head is missing. Height 84 cm., breadth 80 cm., depth 30 cm. M.A.N.

183 GROUP OF MATRONAE, FROM VERTILLUM (Côte-d'Or). Seated on a bench, the trinity of mother-goddesses are shown full-face, in Gallo-Roman style. One holds a baby in swaddling-clothes (important evidence for Gallo-Roman customs in this respect), the middle one holds the swaddling-bands ready, the third a sponge and bowl of water. The one holding the baby has her legs crossed. Native stone, 38 cm. high, 42½ cm. wide, 16½ cm. deep. Relief stands out 14 cm. Musée de Chatillor-sur-Seine. Côte d'Or.

184–5 TWO STATUES OF HORSEMAN OVERCOMING GIANT. This type of group occurs only in Gaul. It typifies the victory of the heavenly powers over the powers of the Underworld which take the form of a crippled giant. It has also been made to symbolize the victory of the Roman Empire over barbarism. 184 is from Portieux (Vosges). Native stone, 1 m. 6 high, 95 cm. long, 37 cm. broad. Musée Epinal. 185 is from Neschers (Puy-de-Dôme). Native stone, 91 cm. high, 77 cm. long, 28 cm. wide, Musée Vichy.

186 GALLIC WARRIOR, FROM VACHÈRES (Basses-Alpes). He wears a shirt of mail, with a torc about his neck, the right hand resting on his sword and the left on his shield. Cloak round his shoulders thrown back. End first century B.C. Native stone. Height 1 m. 60, but the lower part of the legs is missing so that scale was more than life-size. The shield is 1 m. 20 high. Breadth 50 cm. Lapidarium Calvet, Avignon.

187 GALLIC WARRIOR, FROM MONDRAGON (Vaucluse). Wearing a fringed cloak, the lower edge of which hangs down over the typical long Celtic shield. Head and right leg are missing, but right foot and left leg and foot preserved. Native stone, 1 m. 80 high, so the complete figure must have been over 2 m.; shield 1 m. 35. Breadth of statue 70 cm. Lapidarium Calvet, Avignon.

188 CELTIC STANDARDS AND WEAPONS ON FRIEZE OF TRIUMPHAL ARCH AT NARBONNE. The boar with bristling hackles and curled tail on the standard, stylized in T-shape, the oval shield and the helmets with lateral spirals are typically Celtic. The frieze of native white sandstone was found in the fortified walls of Porte de Peripignan. Overall dimensions—height 45 cm., length 1 m. 35, depth 37 cm. This detail 58 cm. long. Musée Regional de l'Histoire de l'Homme Narbonne.

189 Horses Head, from Eysses (Lot-et-Garonne). The mane, stylized into a geometrical pattern, shows two holes which allowed a square-section rod to pass through the head. It was therefore probably a model hobby-horse, or a rocking-horse. The skull form is of 'classical' Arab type. Bronze, 10 cm. high, 17 cm. long, 6½ cm. wide. Musée Agen, Lot-en-Garonne.

190 Hunting God, from Touget (Gers). Though dating only from Gallo-Roman times, this statue, which shows the god in ritual nakedness, with only a cloak over the shoulders, bears many traces of Celtic tradition. He holds a hare in his hands. His dog at his left foot looks up to his face. Stylized face and swept-back hair are Celtic features. Native stone, 75 cm. high, 28 cm. broad, 17½ cm. deep. Musée des Antiquités Nationales.

191 Hare-hunting Relief, from Lutetia (Paris). This frieze in three parts shows on the right a boy cheering several dogs on to the hares, which they are driving into a net. Compare the toils for deer in 96. Limestone. Height 50 cm., length overall 3 m. 25 (1 m.—95 cm.—1 m. 30), depth 18 cm., relief standing out 8 cm. Musée Cluny, Paris.

192 Relief with Head of Hind, from Vindonissa (Aargau). Technique of this fragment is primitive, chipped out rather than carved. In the presentation of the head it maintains the heavily stylized tradition of Celtic animal statues. The protruding tongue of the hind shows that she is being hunted. Native stone, 22 cm. high, 33 cm. wide, 5 cm. deep. Shallow (barely 1 cm.) relief. Vindonissa Museum, Brugg (Switzerland).

193 Relief of Cock and Boar. One side of an altar. Framed in a rich scroll-work of tendrils, a cock above on a plain base and under it on a plinth a boar. *Gallus* (cock) is a Latin pun for Gaul, while the boar was sacred to the Gauls. Stone 1 m. 17 high, 75–82 cm. wide, 67–78 cm. deep. Relief 69 × 40. Avignon.

194 Bronze Pony from Aventicum (Canton de Vaud). An example of the blending in Gallo-Roman times of Celtic tradition with a technical ability, refined by Romanization but also tending to sentimentality. This is brought out by comparison with a 'pure' Celtic animal sculpture like the older 53 above. Height 5½ cm., length 7.7 cm. Musée de l'Histoire de l'Art, Geneva.

195 Running Dog, from Moudon (Canton de Vaud). This model too shows the continuation of Celtic tradition in Gallo-Roman times. The attitude has been distorted by the loss of the hind legs: when the statuette was entire the back did not fall away so steeply to the rear. Bronze, 5½ cm. high, 12 cm. long. Historical Museum, Berne.

196 Relief of Attis Reclining, from Glanum. The consort of Cybele is shown as a shepherd asleep in a landscape, a Phrygian cap on his head, a flowing mantle round his shoulders, hiding with his right hand either his nakedness or his shameful punishment, a curved staff in his left hand and further attributes either hanging on the tree or else incorporated into the design regardless of heaviness. Stylistically this might be taken as the type of Celtic treatment of a Hellenistic Mediterranean theme. Second century B.C. Marble. Height 24½ cm. Width 35 cm. Depth 5 cm. Relief ½ cm. deep. Musée de St-Rémy-de-Provence.

197 Plinths with Human Figure, Animal and Plant Ornament, from Trier. This pair of reliefs shows the clash of Celtic treatment with Roman form, in the human figure which over-emphasizes the head, the much surer drawing of the animal outlines, and more especially in the bold convulutions of the twigs, contrasted with the stiff geometric palm leaves and S-shaped ornaments. On the left side of the back of the upper stone are two birds (ravens?), on the right side a stag. The lower stone is only carved on the front face. It measures 64½ cm. high, 5½ cm. broad, 46 cm. deep, area of relief 29 cm. high, 50 cm. wide. Rheinisches Landesmuseum, Trier.

198 HEAD OF A HELVETIAN, FROM AVENTICUM (Canton de Vaud). Apparently part of a bronze relief. It is one of the most impressive representations of the human face that we have for this period. Height 15½ cm., breadth 12 cm., depth 13 cm. Avenches Museum, Switzerland.

199 SEATED FEMALE FIGURE, FROM MARTIGNY (Valais). This was a table-leg, having its upper part in the form of a woman holding a bowl of fruit while the lower end was an animal's foot. It shows how in the detail of small carvings on objects of everyday domestic use Celtic features influenced the representation of Roman fertility goddesses. The lower surface of the table top rested on the strong metal spike that protrudes to the rear. Height 20·8 cm., width 6 cm. Musée de l'Histoire de l'Art, Geneva.

200–1 FACING-TILE, FROM VINDONISSA (Aargau). Known as antefixes, these tiles at the end of a curved row are still stylized in the antique manner, though late in date, partly because the medium lends itself stylization, an unmistakably Celtic trait. 200 is the head of a Helvetic tribesman, recognizable by his beard and hair-style, and the high-set ears. 201 is a woman's head with neck-ring. The band wound round the forehead falls down to the shoulders either side of the face. 200 measures 21 cm. high, 20 cm. broad, 2 cm. deep. 201 is 19 cm. × 18 cm. × 2 cm. Vindonissa Museum, Brugg, Switzerland.

202 BUST OF A NATIVE GODDESS, FROM AVENTICUM (Vaud). Reproduced here for the sake of the characteristic Gallo-Roman hair-style. The hair is parted from forehead to top-knot and swept back from the face in small locks, then plaited in spiral knots above the nape. Left and right of the neck loose plaits hang down to the shoulders. Probably a Gallic rendering of Venus. The face shows clear traces of Celtic influence. Native bronze work, 21 cm. high, 16 cm. broad. Depth including hair-knot 10½ cm. Avenches Museum, Switzerland.

203 BUST OF GALLIC WOMAN, FROM ALEIA. Also bronze, first century A.D. Shows how Roman hair-styles became fashionable among Gaulish women. The quadruple wave over the crown and the loose plait falling over the nape are typical of Roman style in Nero's time. Height 21 cm., width 12 cm., depth 8 cm. Musée Alesia, Alise-St-Reine.

204 HERM OF GERMANIC BODYGUARD, FROM WELSCHBILLIG (Rhineland). This head, mounted on a pillar, shows in features, hair-style and neck-ornament, a thoroughly un-Roman appearance, as the model must have struck the Roman or Romano-Celtic artist. It also bears witness to the respect which these barbarians in Roman service commanded. Overall height 1 m. 30., breadth 28½ cm. Depth 29 cm. Head alone 35½ cm. high, 21 cm. wide, 23 cm. deep. Rheinisches Landesmuseum, Trier.

205 HERM OF ROMAN GENERAL, SAME SITE. This is a senior officer of the Roman Army but the short, thick neck, and style of hair dressing and beard combined with the somewhat uncouth and forceful expression may indicate that he is by origin a Treveric tribesman and not a true Italian-born Roman. Measurements 1 m. 36 high, 30 cm. broad, 27 cm. deep. Head alone, 39 cm. high, 25 cm. broad, 29 cm. deep (the beard protrudes slightly beyond the front face of the pillar). Rheinisches Landesmuseum, Trier.

206 VETERINARY SURGEON, FROM NANCY. Funeral monument. Gallo-Roman clothing. The deceased holds a 'hipposandal' in his left hand. Roman veterinary practice was to use these for securing dressings on injuries to the sole of the hoof. The face shows traditional Celtic features. Stone, 1 m. 12 high, 79 cm. broad, 21 cm. deep. Relief stands out 15 cm. Musée Nancy.

207 HORSE-DEALER, FROM DIJON. This relief was found in the town. The dealer wears a hooded cloak as used by peasants. In front of him are two horses, the lower part of one only scored out. He carries a stick in his right hand. Behind the horses another man (his groom?) brandishes a whip. The whole block measures 1 m. 10 high, 66 cm. broad, 60½ cm.

deep. Relief surface 50 × 65, 2 cm. deep. Archaeological Museum, Dijon.

208 VARIOUS GALLO-ROMAN VEHICLES, FROM NEAR VAISON (Vaucluse). Below, diligence or omnibus. Four-wheeler, drawn by a pair of horses abreast. Passengers both inside and on top. The driver on the box is just giving a cut with his whip. Details of harness and coachwork are fairly clear. Above, two racing chariots as used in the games at the circus or hippodrome. Local stone, 1 m. 40 high, 1 m. 36 to 1 m. 43 wide. Lapidarium Calvet, Avignon.

209 SAILING SHIP AND CHARIOT, FROM JUENKERATH (Rhineland). Dyptich, badly damaged but still showing a mariner hoisting sail below, and, above, part of a chariot with the driver in the narrow space between the wheel and the horse's croup, holding the reins, with a passenger above and behind him. Local stone, 1 m. 11 high, 73 cm. wide, 19 cm. deep, relief stands out 4 cm. Rheinisches Landesmuseum, Trier.

210 RIVER-BARGE BEING TOWED, CABRIÈRES-D'AYGUES (Vaucluse). The barge is laden with two wine-casks and hauled by three men on the tow-path; only two men in the picture. Steersman sitting aft of casks. Above, design of three *fiaschi* and four jugs with handles. Relief on local stone. Height 63 cm., length. 1 m. 49. Length of ship 85 cm. Lapidarium Calvet, Avignon, Vaucluse.

211 MAN TOWING BARGE, DETAIL OF 210 ABOVE. The one in the middle.

212 THE FAMOUS MOSELLE BARGE, FROM NIJMWEGEN (Rhineland). This is the most significant evidence we have, and the most striking for the construction of boats and the technique of barge traffic in the Gallo-Roman period. First half of third century A.D. Height 1 m. 53, length 3 m. 5, width 63 cm. This detail 1 m. 40 high, 1 m. 5 long. Provincial Museum, Trier.

213 FUDDLED COXWAIN OF MOSELLE BARGE, NIJMWEGEN. This famous study, so expressive of vinous bliss, comes from the tombstone of a wine-merchant at Trier. The head, using the cask as a pillow, is 19 cm. high, 15 cm. wide, 17 cm. deep.

214 CLOGMAKER IN HIS WORKSHOP, FROM RHEIMS. This tombstone shows the craftsman at work, an example of how in Gallo-Roman times a man's trade accompanied him to the grave and beyond. Local stone. Height 1 m. 10, breadth 76 cm. Rheims Museum.

215 PRICING A BOLT OF CLOTH, RELIEF FROM HIRZWEILER (Rhineland). This also is a tombstone presenting the tradesman at his business. Behind the draper and his customer with the dress-length spread out between them are seen further rolled and corded bolts.

216 PAYING TAXES, RELIEF FROM NIJMWEGEN (Rhineland). This scene is one of the most significant pictures of social life in the Gallo-Roman era. Notice the emphatic difference between the bearded, hooded peasant in the background and the shaven *publicanus* at his money-laden table, sitting at the receipt of custom. Height 60 cm., breadth 1 m. 39½, 52 cm. deep. Our detail (there were two other tax-collectors right and left) is 60 cm. high, 86 cm. broad, relief 11 cm. Provincial Museum, Trier.

217 PASTRYCOOK'S STALL, RELIEF FROM METZ. Here we have a lively picture of the confectioner, sitting with his pastries before him on the counter while the customer makes his own selection of sweetmeats from the boxes above. Late second century A.D. Height 89 cm., depth of relief 5 cm. Metz Museum.

218 MEMORIAL TO CHILDREN AT ARLON (Belgium). Three faces of this tombstone were worked. On the front a Gallo-Roman married couple stand hand in hand; the left side also shows a man and a woman; on the right face above the parents sitting at table have unfortunately been destroyed (three out of four missing), while below the children share their meal with a dog. To the left of the squatting children their elder sister supervises the younger ones, while facing her a boy plays the flute, an instrument proper to funerals. End of second century A.D. Found at Arlon. Overall height 107 cm., breadth 80 cm., depth 70½ cm.; this detail 53 × 64, relief 5 cm. deep. Metz Museum.

219 Head of Medusa, from Labarthe-Inard (Haute-Garonne). This fragment of relief belongs to a tombstone and depicts the gorgon's head so often associated with death, because it turns the beholder to stone. The Classical motif here bears traces, in the triangle of scarf under the round chin, of Celtic geometrical stylization. Limestone, 65 cm. high, 49 cm. broad. Musée Communal, Martres-Tolosane (Haute-Garonne).

220 Ex-Voto, from the Source of the Seine. This is an offering from a pilgrim to the shrine of Sequana, showing the pilgrim himself with his ritual gift, some kind of fruit, in his hand. Head and shoulders Gallo-Roman with clearly Celtic features. Stone. Height 82½ cm., breadth 32 cm., depth 14 cm. Depth of relief 7½ cm. Archaeological Museum, Dijon.

221 Ex-Voto, from the Source of the Seine. Figure of a child, worked fully in the round, wearing a hooded cloak. It too is a pilgrim, carrying a puppy in both hands. Stone. Height 59 cm., breadth of plinth 21 cm., depth 18 cm. Archaeological Museum Dijon.

222 Blind Child, from the Source of the Seine. Among the offerings found in the shrine this figure is a most striking representation of human suffering, a child led to the healing nature-goddess by pilgrims. The treatment of the face still owes much to Celtic tradition. Stone, 19½ cm. high, 10½ cm., broad, 3½ cm. deep. Archaeological Museum, Dijon.

223 Cinerary Urn with Two Human Busts, from Arnesp (Haute-Garonne). Probably a husband (right) and wife (left), under two arches between stylized Corinthian columns. The upper part of the body sketchily indicated, the almost schematized heads are typical Celtic treatments of form. The work was found in the necropolis beside a Roman temple on the site of which a priory was founded in the Middle Ages. Marble, 51 cm. high, 38 cm. broad, 69 cm. deep. In private ownership.

224 Head of a Sick Man, from Alesia. This head, which was probably an ex-voto, was shown to a professor of medicine who was able to diagnose a disease of the bone from symptoms reproduced in the carving. Thus Romano-Celtic art can even tell us something about the ills the Gallic provincials suffered from. Stone, 22½ cm. high, 16½ cm. broad, 11 cm. deep. Musée Communal, Alise-Ste-Reine.

225 Recumbent Gaul, from Alesia. This bronze appliqué represents the clothing (breeches, boots, and belt) affected by the Gauls. The man seems to be asleep, with his head propped on his right forearm. Some authorities have taken this to be a dead or wounded warrior, but this is unlikely in view of the relaxed posture of the body. Height 10 cm., breadth 3 cm., depth 2 cm. Musée Alesia.

Pioneers of Christianity

226 The Avenue of Tombs at Les Aliscamps at Arles. At the time of the Roman occupation the Via Aurelia to the east of Arles was lined with richly decorated pagan tombs. From the fourth century A.D. onwards a Christian necropolis sprang up which by the early Middle Ages had grown into the biggest cemetery in the West. The costly sculptured sarcophagi are mostly distributed in various museums. The Christian lapidarium at Arles luckily preserves a considerable number of these monuments of which the pictures below have been taken. Along the noble avenues of Aliscamps stand simple stone coffins which still retain lids in the style of the Greek sarcophagus. In the background the ruins of the Church of St Honorat, which was a considerable resort of pilgrims from the fifth century onwards.

227–8 Sarcophagus, from La Gayole (Var). So called from its original site. 227—detail—rather more than a third, to the badly damaged perforated centre—from the right side as the viewer sees it. On the left-hand side the Good Shepherd, carrying a young ram on his shoulders, turned towards the seated figure on the right. Half visible behind his legs, also facing right, a second ram. On the right a seated male figure, the significance of which is still disputed, with the right hand raised in greeting, the left hand holding a staff, possibly a shepherd's crook. A lamb behind the seat. Between the two bearded figures in Greek garb, a tree, in the crown of which sits a bird also turned towards the seated figure. 228: the left half of the sarcophagus shows from left to right: bust representing the sun, still in pagan form; a fisherman with rod and line (St Peter?); rams and lambs in front of a tree with a bird facing right; a woman praying in the traditional suppliant attitude, a sheep behind her. Third century. In the sixth century adapted for use as the tomb of Syagria, foundress of the Merovingian chapel of La Gayole which is still standing. Marble from Asia Minor, overall dimensions 81 cm. high, 2 m. 22 long (back of sarcophagus has not survived). Parish church of Brignoles, Var.

229 Early Christian Altar with Chi-Rho Monogram and Phoenix. In the lower shallow relief occur the superimposed letters from the name of Christ, corresponding to Kh and Rh, more faintly sketched towards the right side. The letters Alpha and Omega (for Beginning and End) depend from the top strokes of the Chi. The phoenix above stands for the Resurrection and at the same time for Christ. Marble, 1 m. 18 high, 49 cm. broad, 32–34 cm. deep. Phoenix 28 cm. high

230 The Laying-on of Hands. That the prayer of the man on the right has been heard is symbolized by the gesture of Christ on the left, who is seen approaching him. This gesture, already a favourite one on Greek steles, is interpreted here in Christian terms, as the granting of grace and the admission into Paradise. Detail from a sarcophagus, overall dimensions of which were height 61 cm., length 2 m. 06, depth 72 cm. Relief alone 52½ cm. high, 36 cm. broad, 5 cm. deep. Crypt of St-Maximin (Var).

231 The Praying Woman of Aliscamps. This sarcophagus is named after the principal figure on it. She stands with her hands spread out in prayer in front of a drapery that hangs in great knots to right and left of her head. On the far left and right stand two apostles as sponsors; at the feet of the woman is a bundle of scrolls. Overall dimensions 55 cm. high, 2 m. 22 long, 66 cm. deep. Female figure alone 47 cm. high, width from hand to hand 30 cm. Christian Lapidarium, Arles.

232 Daniel, from the Sarcophagus Lid of Pascasia. Daniel stands between two lions, in a suppliant attitude, as symbol of Christian steadfastness. The prophet Habbakuk tenders him a round loaf, the Eucharist. Angel to the left of Daniel. Carrara marble, overall 35½ cm. high, 162 cm. long. Scene alone 29 cm. high, 37 cm. wide. Christian Lapidarium, Arles.

233 Adam and Eve, from the Same Lid. Standing on either side of the Tree of Knowledge, holding in their hands leaves to cover their nakedness. The angel is pushing Eve out of Paradise. No serpent. The animal beside Eve is a sheep, symbol of the burden of work laid on the ancestors of mankind. Carrara marble, detail 29 cm. high, 40 cm. broad. Christian Lapidarium, Arles.

234 Peter Baptizing the Roman Centurion Cornelius. Scene from the sarcophagus of Anastasia or of Constantine II. Behind Cornelius a Roman legionary pointing to him, as he emulates Moses by striking a rock with this staff to release a spring of salvation. In the conventions of the sarcophagus Cornelius stands for the conversion of the Roman world to Christianity. Carrara marble, Overall height 59 cm., length 2 m. 18, depth 75 cm. Detail 59 × 68. Christian Lapidarium, Arles.

235 The Israelites after the Crossing of the Red Sea. The sea has closed up behind them. In the marching column of Israelites are a blind man led by two companions and a child hand in hand with an adult. This scene has given its name to the sarcophagus. Overall height 73 cm., length 2 m. 28, depth 1 m. This detail 34 × 52. Christian Lapidarium, Arles.

236 Three Wise Men at the Manger. The Magi wear Phrygian caps; they are not yet thought of as kings. With their gifts they approach the manger, behind which stand an ox and a he-goat. On the other side of the manger stands Mary, deep in thought. The Star hangs between her head and the roof of the stable. To the right, one of the heads which in late Roman times replaced the acroteria of classical sarcophagi. Dimensions overall—30 cm. high, 2 m. 20 long, 65–75 cm. deep. Carved area 24½ × 71, relief 2½ cm. deep. Crypt of St-Maximin (Var).

237 The Innocents Brought before Herod. Scene from the same coffin-lid as 236. The seated king confronted by two executioners and a mother who stands in an attitude of affliction, her hands pressed to her heart. Carving 24½ cm. high, 54 cm. long. Crypt of St-Maximin (Var).

238 Three Wise Men below the Manger. Scene from the Sarcophagus of the Shepherds and the Magi. The manger in the upper plane. Mary sitting to left, shepherd standing to right, ox and ass behind crib, the Star above Mary. In the lower plane the three Magi in Phrygian caps, pointing up at the crib. Compare the vertical grouping of the figures with the horizontal grouping in 236. Marble from St-Beat. Overall height 54 cm., length 2 m. 22, depth 73 cm. Carving 47 × 27/30. Christian Lapidarium, Arles.

239 Pastoral Scene, from a Sarcophagus Lid. Between two trees from which a pan-pipes and a wallet hang, a shepherd with three sheep (the Good Shepherd). On the right an acroterion head. On left a winged, naked Cupid, holding the central plate (tessera) in traditional antique style: in this case it bears no inscription. Carrara marble. Height overall 28 cm., length 1 m. 95, depth 68 cm. Carving alone, without border, 23½ cm. × 90 cm. Christian Lapidarium, Arles.

240 The Sacrifice of Abraham. From the same sarcophagus as 238. Outer vignette on right. Abraham has placed his left hand on the head of the kneeling Isaac. In his right hand, ready to strike, he holds the sacrificial knife, or sword, which has been partly broken off. To his right, exactly as described in the Old Testament, a young ram is hanging by its horns from a bush. Above the bush the hand of the angel, restraining Abraham from carrying out the sacrifice. Overall measurements as in 238. Carving alone 34 cm. high, 27 cm. wide. Christian Lapidarium, Arles. (Compare the engraved marble slab from from St-Maximin with same theme.)

241 The Daughter of Zairus Awakened, from the Sarcophagus of Christ's Departure. Christ has taken the daughter by the hand, to raise her up. Behind her the father leans on the back of the couch. Her mother has prostrated herself at the feet of Christ. Marble from Prokonnes. Overall dimensions 70 cm. high, 2 m. 26 cm. (restored) long, depth of surviving side of coffin 11 cm. Carving alone 60 cm. high, 1 m. wide. Christian Lapidarium, Arles.

242 Baptism of Cornelius, from Sarcophagus of the Miraculous Spring. So-called on account of this carving. This is the same subject as in 234. Here the Roman officer kneels low before Peter and begs him for baptism. Behind him a legionary points to the apostle. The cap worn by the Roman soldiers is of the kind called a 'pileus'. Carrara marble. Overall 59 cm. high, 2 m. 21 long, depth of surviving wall 21 cm. Christian Lapidarium, Arles.

243 The Miracle of the Loaves and Fishes. The 'eucharistic' sarcophagus. Figures in niches, lightly divided by archways, with Christ in the centre in very high relief; one apostle bringing loaves from the left, another fish from the right. St-Béat marble. Overall 64 cm. high, 2 m. 05 long, 73 cm. deep. Scene alone 57 × 85. Christian Lapidarium, Arles.

244 Christ Working Miracle. Trees, from which this sarcophagus takes its name, with birds sitting in the branches, divide the space into niches. Left and right of a suppliant female figure Christ appears three times on each side working miracles. Our detail shows the raising of the widow's son at Naim; the healing of the woman with an issue of blood; the loaves and fishes. The other miracles are the wedding at Cana, the healing of the man born blind and of the lame man. Prokonnes marble. 71 cm. high, 2 m. 33 long, 84 cm. deep. Carving alone, 60 cm. × 1 m. Christian Lapidarium, Arles.

245 Christ Foretelling His Betrayal to Peter. Scene from the 'Peter sarcophagus' at St-Maximin. In the next carving to the right the cock is seen standing in the crown of a palm tree, crowing. In the central carving it is standing under the raised hand of Christ. Peter, abashed, clutches his beard. Overall dimensions 55½ cm. high, 2 m. 22 long, 72 cm. deep. Carving alone, 50 cm. high, 87 cm. broad, depth of relief 6 cm. Crypt of St-Maximin (Var).

246 The Raising of the Dead and the Giving of Keys to Peter, from a Sarcophagus Lid at St-Maximin. The stereotyped reproduction of the figure of Christ in the two scenes is most striking. Only the attitude of the hands is slightly different in each. Overall 47 cm. high, 2 m. 11 long, thickness of surviving wall 10 cm. Carving without border 32 x 67, relief 3½ cm. deep. Crypt of St-Maximin (Var).

247 Apostle's Head, from the Sarcophagus of Anastasis. The apostles are shown approaching from left and right across, above which was once a Chi-Rho monogram, surrounded by a wreath. Stars and clouds behind their heads represent heaven. Overall dimensions as in 234. This detail 35 cm. high, 30 cm. broad. Christian Lapidarium, Arles.

248 Figures of Apostles from the Sarcophagus of Concordius. The principle façade of the coffin shows Christ as the giver of the Law (Dominus legem dat), surrounded by evangelists, apostles and the faithful. Our picture shows the third and the fourth figure to the right of Christ. Overall dimensions: height 60 cm., length 2 m. 19, depth 80 cm.; this detail: height 35 cm., breadth 30 cm. Christian Lapidarium, Arles.

249 Heads of Apostles, from 242. These are the heads of the figures standing second and third from the left of the suppliant woman. They are looking directly into each other's eyes, as if in earnest conversation. Overall dimensions as in 242. Height of heads 9 and 10 cm. respectively. Christian Lapidarium, Arles.

250 Meleager's Hunt, from a Sarcophagus in the Christian Cemetery at St-Sernin, Toulouse. Here we have a figure from classical mythology, the hunter of the Boar of Calydon, flanked by Castor and Pollux. The central motif, the overcoming of the monster, is interpreted in Christian eyes as the victory of good over evil. Fifth or sixth century A.D. White marble, 51 cm. high, 2 m. long, 58 cm. deep. The central portion takes in exactly one-third of the whole front panel. Augustinian Museum, Toulouse.

251 Baptistry of Aix-en-Provence. Circular building, on the south side of the cathedral next to the second and third cross-vaultings of the romanesque part of the fabric, with floor 90 cm. lower than the latter. Octagonal with quadrangular ambulatory, borne by eight pillars alternately of cipolino and granite with marble bases and corinthian capitals of second or third century, probably taken from a temple. Original floor in centre, with octagonal font. Main structure end of fourth or early fifth century. The upper part with its cupola and stuccos is sixteenth century. Diameter of octagon, 12 m. 70. Font 1 m. 60, depth 95 cm.

252 Marble Slab with Lamb, Autun (Saone-et-Loire). Freehand drawing with a minimum of lines of the Lamb of God, a branch, and grapes. Slab damaged at upper side, but the greater part of the ornamental border has been preserved. The confident proportions, the elegance of the head and the hoofs bear witness to the rare ability of an artist standing midway between late antiquity and the early middle ages. Fifth century A.D. Height 65 cm., breadth 60–2, depth 7 cm. Musée Rollin, Autun.

253 MARBLE SLAB, SACRIFICE OF ABRAHAM. Abraham, on very large scale, not quite in the middle of the slab, his left hand on Isaac's head, his right hand raised to strike, upper edge unfortunately destroyed. On either side of his legs the ram and the altar of sacrifice. The feet of the figures come outside the border. Sixth century A.D. Height 76 cm., breadth 66, depth 3 cm. Crypt of St-Maximin (Var).

254 TOMBSTONE WITH GRAPES AND FISHES, TOULOUSE. Probably the front panel of a cinerary urn. The ornamentally treated bird's heads, pecking at the grapes with the temple door above them, form the original, severely geometrical, relief. Presumably in Christian times the fishes at left and right were added in a much more primitive style, so that the old pagan monument could be rehabilitated by the Christian IKHTHUS (Fish) symbol. St-Béat marble, 51 cm. high, 45 cm. broad, 7 cm. deep. Augustinian Museum, Toulouse.

255 CONSTANTINIAN CHI-RHO MONOGRAM FLANKED BY DOVES, FROM MARSEILLES. Detail of an altar-table, decorated all round, from the Abbey of St Victor at Marseilles. Frieze-like design running round four sides and comprising twelve doves and also the Lamb of God surrounded by twelve sheep. Rows of vines between the birds. Fifth century A.D. Carrara marble. Overall dimensions 18 cm. high, 1 m. 77 long, 1 m. 12 broad. This detail 65 cm. long. Musée Borely, Marseilles.

256 THE LAMB OF THE APOCALYPSE WITH THE BOOK OF SEVEN SEALS, FROM SAIGNON (Vaucluse). Left part of a relief. But for the Greek inscription to be seen above on the right of our detail one could easily take this picture for early Romanesque work, especially the averted head. It is, however, early Christian and midway between the late Classical and the beginnings of medieval art. In the geometrical stylized lines of the animal's body the Celtic heritage is still dominant. Overall dimensions: height 55 cm., length 87 cm., depth of stone not measurable. Our detail: height 22.5 cm., breadth 36 cm., depth of the relief 3 cm. Parish church, Saignon.

257 CHI-RHO MONOGRAM ON EARLY CHRISTIAN SARCOPHAGUS AT MARTRES-TOLOSANES (Haute-Garonne). This carving from an early Christian cemetery presents the culmination of late classical art in the service of the new faith, both in the delicately drawn amalgamated letters, making much play with curves above and below the nexus and the ornamental foliage, treated in the matter of a ceiling cornice, to right and left; and still the drawing shows traces of the Celtic geometrical style. Fifth century A.D. St-Béat marble. Overall 48 cm. high, 2 m. 12 long, 63 cm. deep. This detail 65 cm. long. Church Martres-Tolosanes.

258 APSE OF ST-JULIEN, NEAR RUSTREL (Vaucluse). The priory, founded according to documentary evidence in the fifth century still includes this magnificently simple end-wall of the nave, still pre-romanesque and lighted only by a single central window. An example of how Roman architectural technique was continued in church building. (The nave itself has fallen in.)

259 THE CHAPEL OF ST-CESAIRE AT VERNEGUES (Bouche-du-Rhône). Built as a lean-to on the ruins of the temple shown in 113 above, out of salvaged fragments of the fabric of the pagan shrine, this tiny Christian church has no monumental flight of steps leading up to a mighty portico before the image of the gods: only a small door opening into an almost windowless nave, where the worship of the living God has outlasted the dead gods and all the fanes erected in their honour, even as the eternal does the temporal.

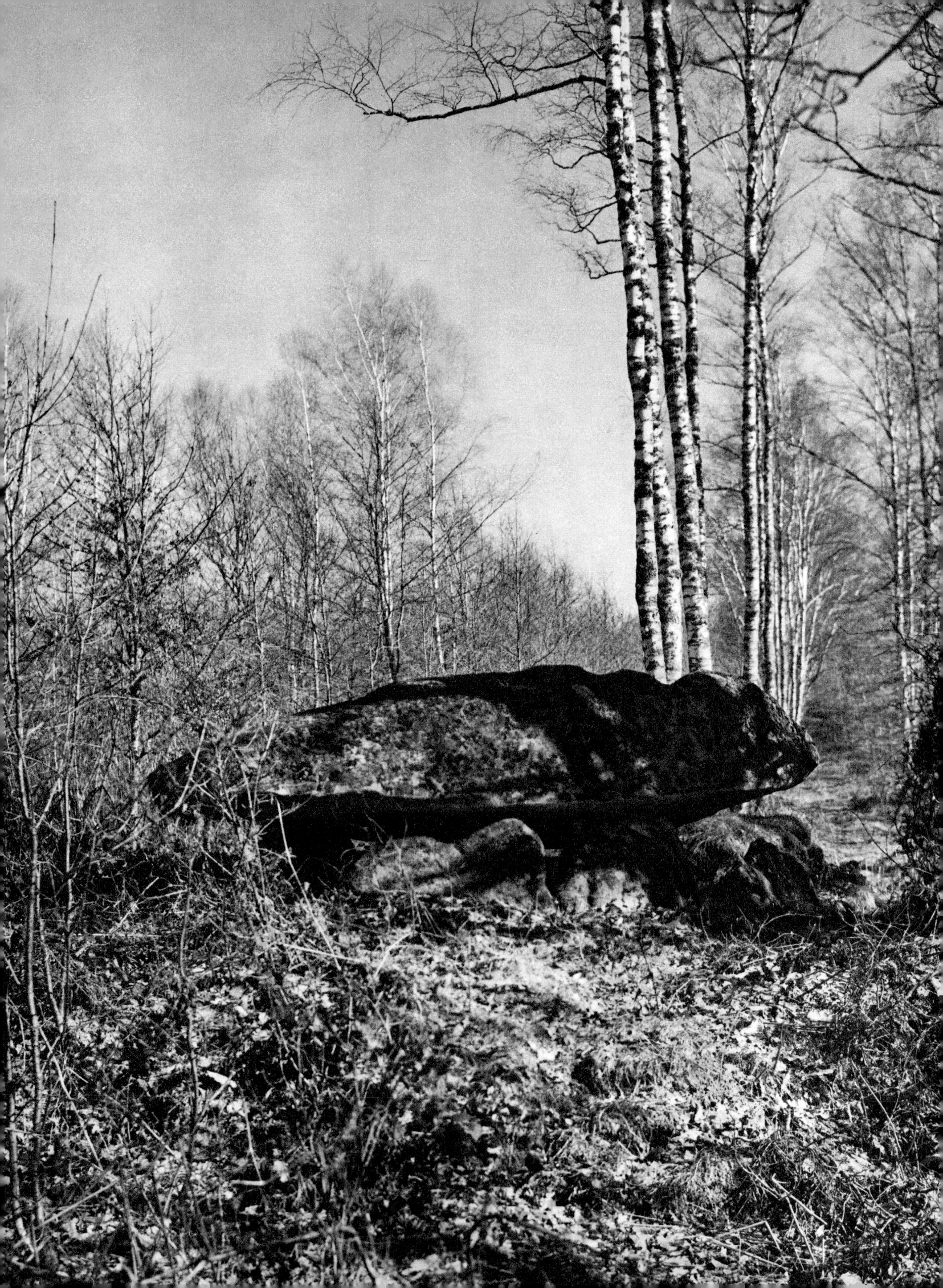

2

4

5

6

7

II

13

14

15

16

19

20

21

25

26

27

28

29

31

32 33

39

41 42

43

44
45

47

48

49 50

51

52

54

19

63

64

67 68

69

70

72

73

79

80

81

82 83

87

88

89

92 93

97

98

101

104 105

111

112

114 I

TOUS LES MONUMENTS

118 ▲

119

12

123

125 I

27 128

129

131

132

133

137

1

138

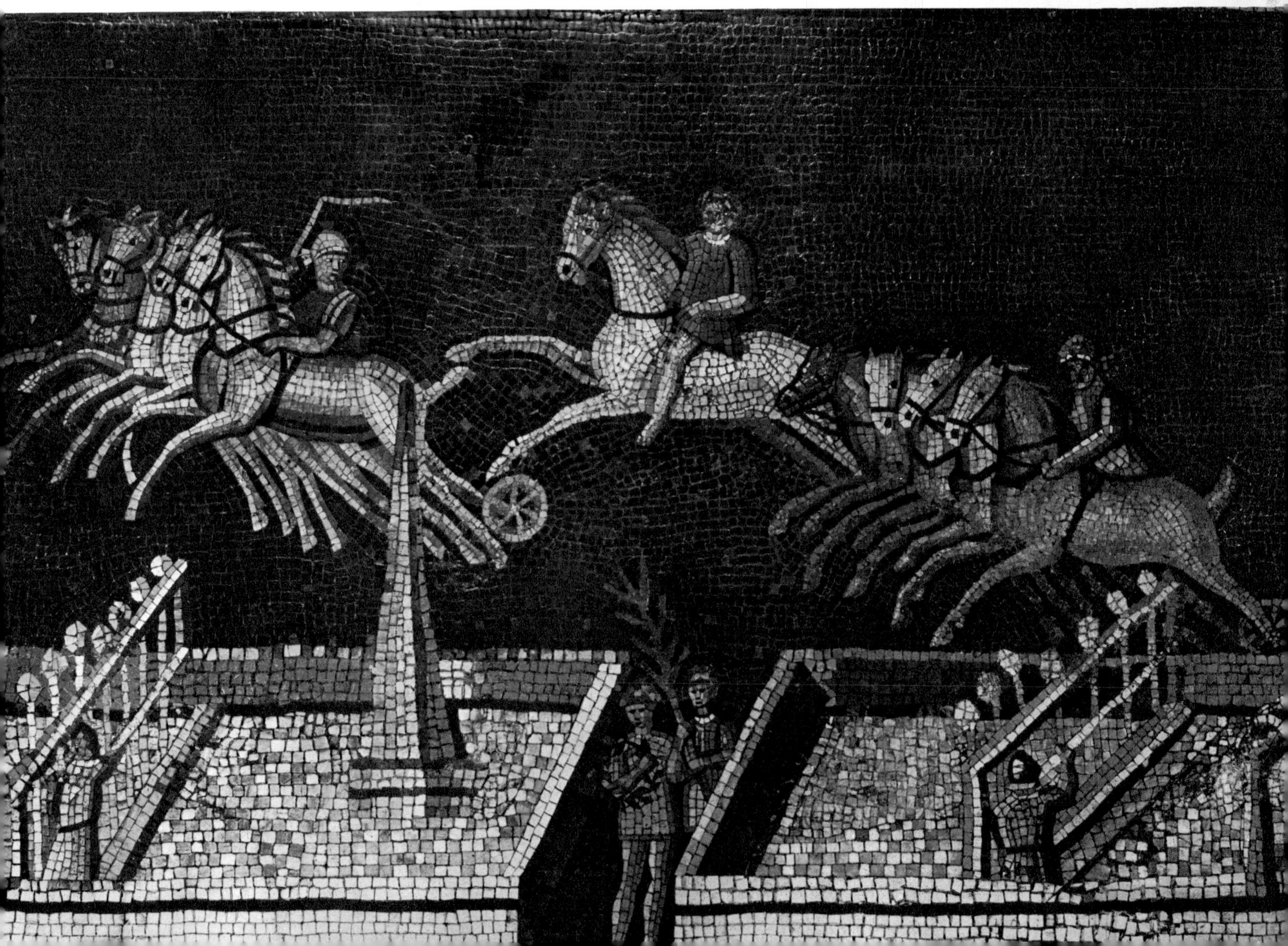

142

I 143

144

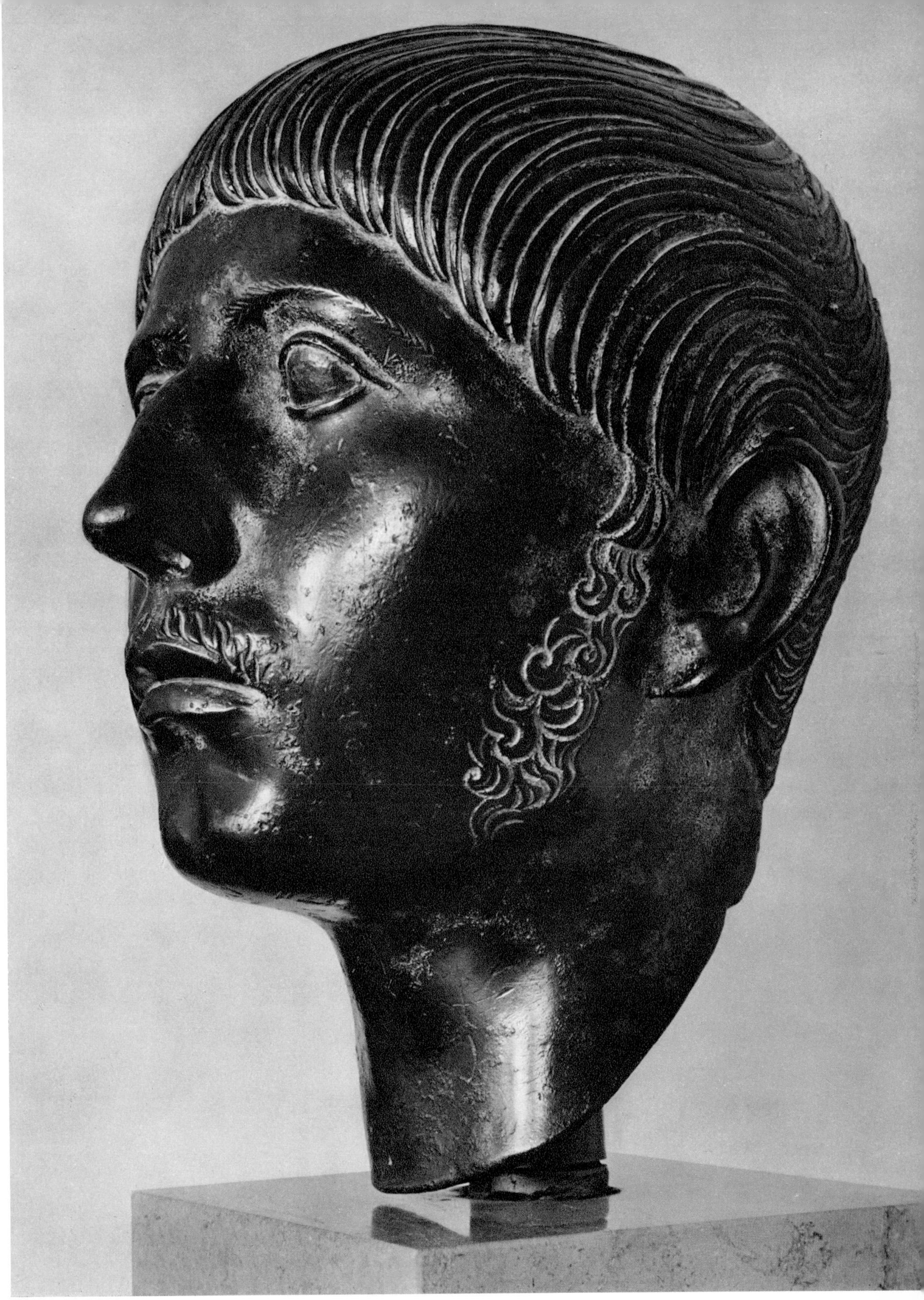

145

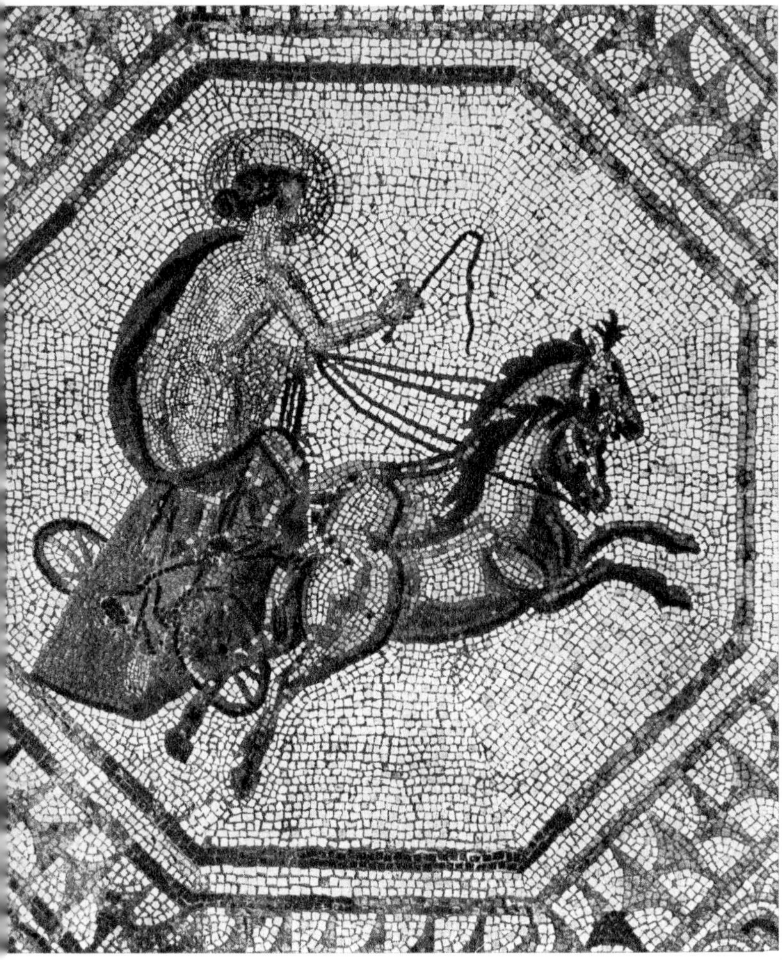

▲ 147 148

149 150

151 152

155

8 159

160

161

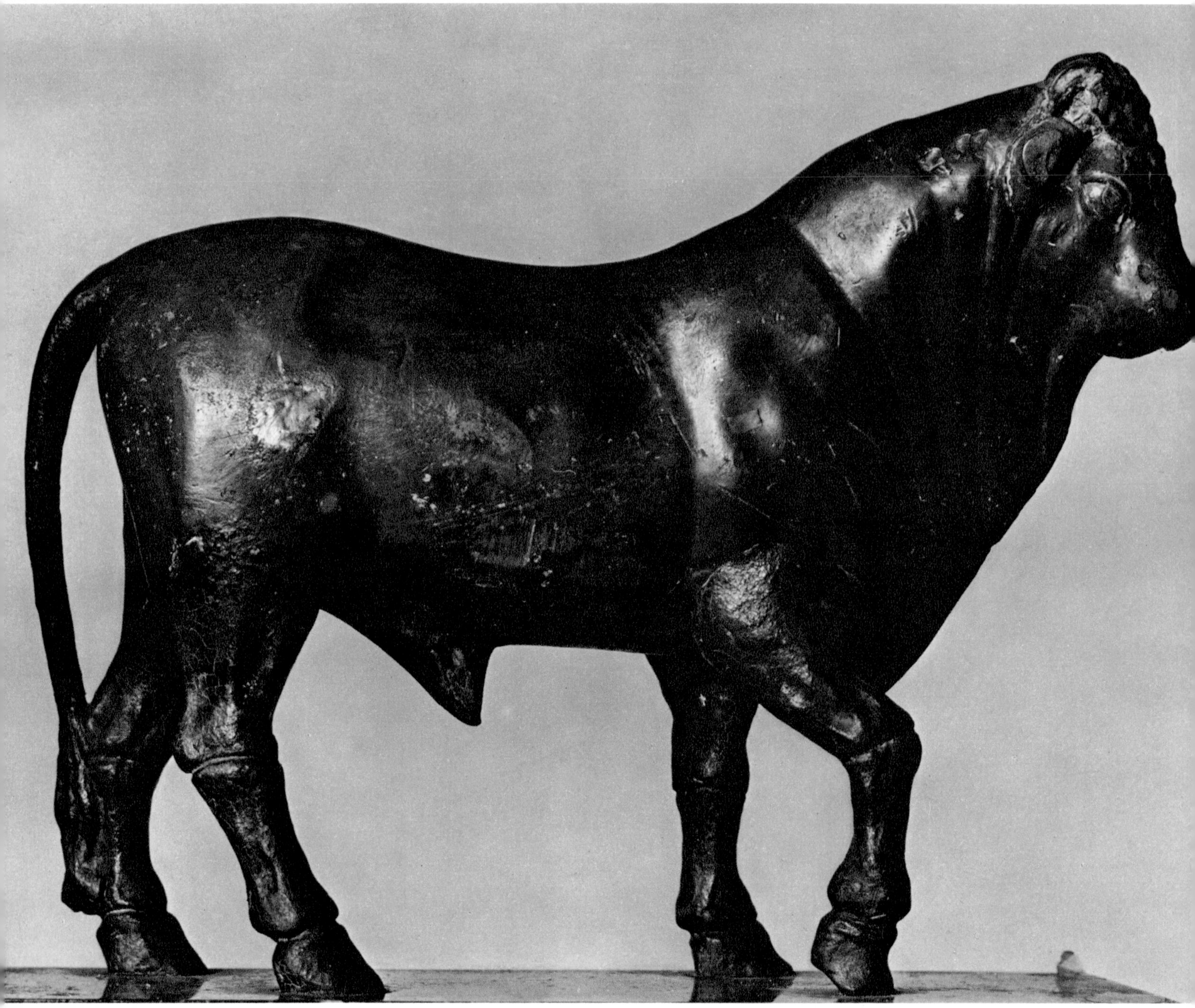

163

164

65 166

167

172

ESVS

3

174

175

176

181

184

185

186 187

188
189

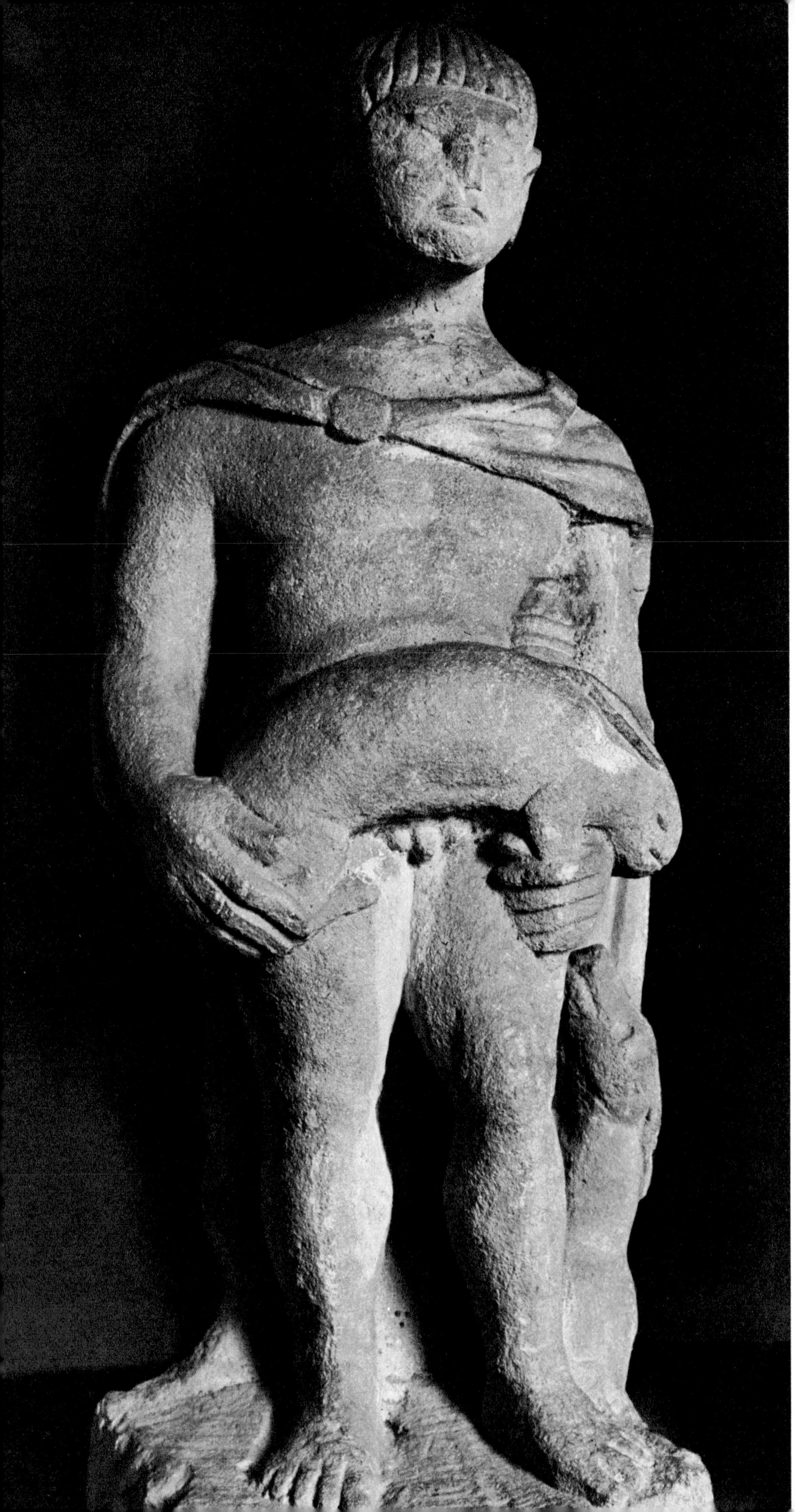

190

193

194

195

199

202

203

204 20

206

209

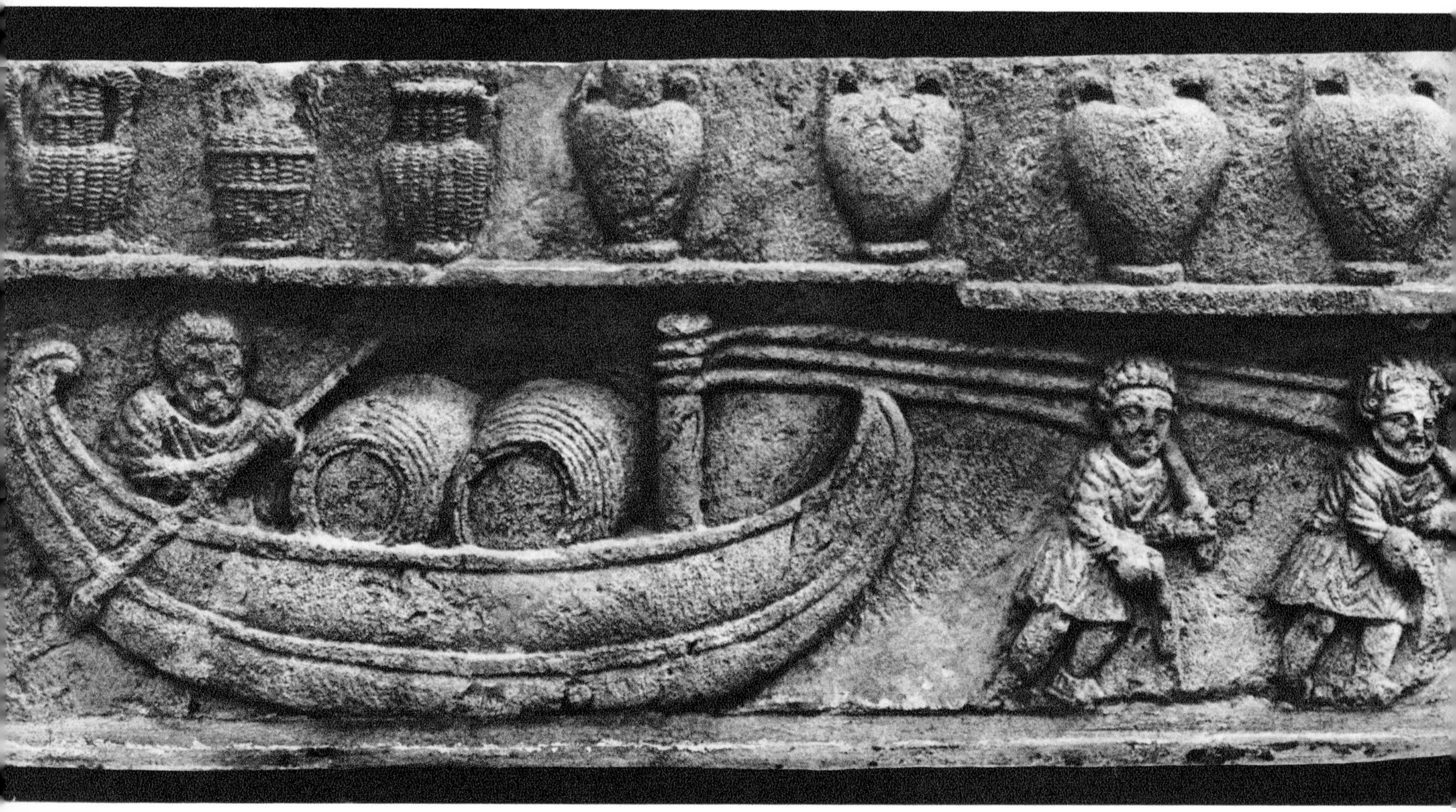

211

212 21

4

6

217

2

218

225

22(

227

22

229

230

231

234

33 235

36 238
37

39
40

242 243

244

245

246

24

248

249

252

253

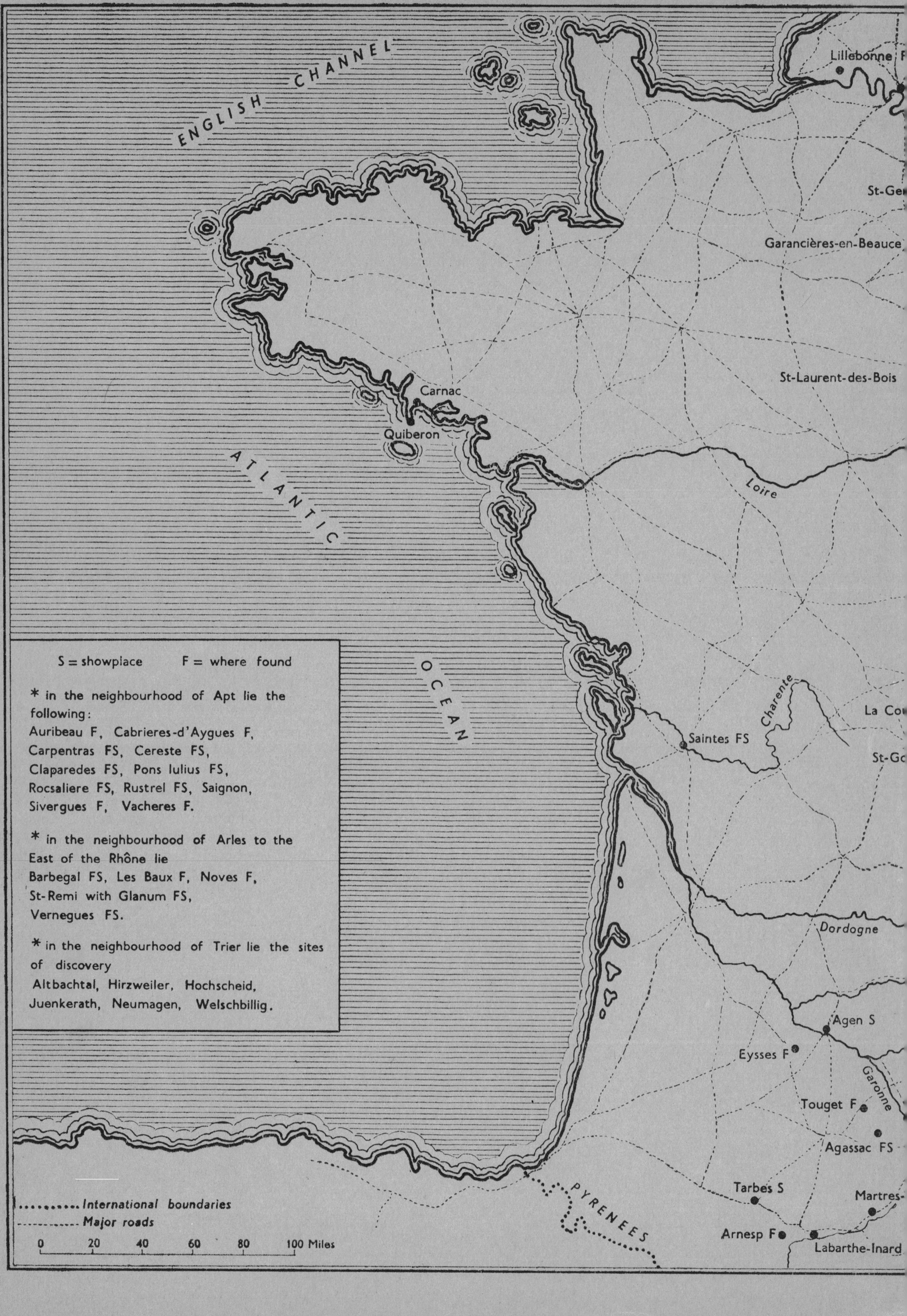

ENGLISH CHANNEL
ATLANTIC OCEAN
Lillebonne F
St-Ge
Garancières-en-Beauce
St-Laurent-des-Bois
Carnac
Quiberon
Loire
Charente
La Co
Saintes FS
St-Go
Dordogne
Agen S
Eysses F
Garonne
Touget F
Agassac FS
Tarbes S
Martres-
Arnesp F
Labarthe-Inard
PYRENEES
S = showplace F = where found
* in the neighbourhood of Apt lie the following:
Auribeau F, Cabrieres-d'Aygues F, Carpentras FS, Cereste FS, Claparedes FS, Pons Iulius FS, Rocsaliere FS, Rustrel FS, Saignon, Sivergues F, Vacheres F.
* in the neighbourhood of Arles to the East of the Rhône lie
Barbegal FS, Les Baux F, Noves F, St-Remi with Glanum FS, Vernegues FS.
* in the neighbourhood of Trier lie the sites of discovery
Altbachtal, Hirzweiler, Hochscheid, Juenkerath, Neumagen, Welschbillig.
International boundaries
Major roads
0 20 40 60 80 100 Miles